Praise for the
AMERICAN
MUSLIM
teenager's
handbook

Winner of the 2008 Arizona Book Award

"*The American Muslim Teenager's Handbook* is a 'must read' . . . for those who want an inside view of Islam and our Muslim youth today. It reveals their faith and its impact on their lives, and the challenges and issues of growing up Muslim in the West."

> —John L. Esposito, founding director of the Center for Muslim-Christian Understanding, and coauthor of *Who Speaks for Islam? What a Billion Muslims Really Think*

"What a delightful, hilarious, wonderful, beautiful book! I loved it!"

> —Reza Aslan, author of *No God but God: The Origins, Evolution, and Future of Islam*

"The empowerment of Muslim youth unleashes a tremendous amount of energy for positive and constructive involvement. I am delighted to see the initiatives of self identity. . . . Congratulations!"

> —Sayyid M. Syeed, national director of the Islamic Society of North America (ISNA)

"I love this book! I bought copies for my nieces and nephews. . . . Heck, I've got a copy for my son, and he's not even two yet."

> —Eboo Patel, executive director of Interfaith Youth Core, and author of *Acts of Faith: The Story of an American Muslim, the Struggle for the Soul of a Generation*

"Filled with basic information about Islam, presented in a straightforward way, [the handbook] then applies these religious truths to the life of a teenager. What a book!"

—Dr. Paul Eppinger, executive director, Arizona Faith Movement

"I believe it is a path-breaking and invaluable window into how some Muslim teens are coping with the challenges of growing up in the west. It is a must-read for all who care about the future of Islam in the West."

—Dr. Jeffrey Lang, author of *Losing My Religion: A Call For Help*

"Being a Muslim teenager in America has become that much easier with the publication of this much-needed and timely book. Written in a highly engaging, nonpreachy style, the handbook offers American Muslim teens answers to practically every question that may occur to them concerning lifestyle issues and religious concerns. Strongly recommended not only for these teenagers but for their parents as well."

—Dr. Asma Afsaruddin, associate professor of Arabic and Islamic Studies, University of Notre Dame

"Congratulations to the Hafiz family on this superb guide to Muslim life in America for teens and their parents! Funny and forthright, *The American Muslim Teenager's Handbook* tackles all the difficult questions about faith that young Muslims face everyday while opening a window into candid and confident interfaith communication. Written with wit, charm, and rare honesty, this book is a must-read for Muslims and non-Muslims alike."

—Ausma Khan, editor in chief, *Muslim Girl* magazine

"*The American Muslim Teenager's Handbook* triumphs in shattering so many of the painful stereotypes about Islam and Muslims that have increasingly infected American society since 9/11. Practical, educational, and entertaining, the book acknowledges the diversity in practice and background among American Muslims today. It holds important lessons for *all* Americans, regardless of age or faith background."

—Melody Moezzi, author of *War on Error: Real Stories of American Muslims*

"What a wonderful insight into the lives of Muslim teens! My Jewish students saw in the experience of their peers parallels to their own religious questions and challenges . . . The Hafiz family has provided a great service . . . Their work begins for us all an ongoing conversation about the role of religion, culture, and community in American society."

—Rabbi Sheila Goloboy, Port Jewish Center, Port Washington, New York

"Every American needs to read this book. It presents, especially for Christian and Jewish young people, an opportunity to gain a desperately needed understanding of the history they share with Muslim young people . . . that can hopefully lead to harmony. . . . It is an important and enlightening asset in promoting peace among all who believe in the One God."

—Dr. Larry Hostetler, founding minister of the Chaparral Christian Church

"For Muslims it is important to be a global citizen and to build bridges of peace . . . [W]orking with Greg Mortenson, whose goal is eradicating global illiteracy, has helped me find harmony and balance in the fast-paced American Muslim life. This book is an invaluable guide to eradicating misunderstandings based on ignorance and fear."

—Sadia Ashraf, outreach coordinator for Central Asia Institute

". . . *The American Muslim Teenager's Handbook* . . . promises to be a vivid and functional guide for many generations of American Muslim teenagers, empowering them both as Americans and as Muslims, and thereby bringing them one step closer to the ideal of the Great American Judeo-Christian-Muslim tradition."

—Ranya Idliby, coauthor of *The Faith Club: A Muslim, A Christian, A Jew—Three Women Search for Understanding*

the
AMERICAN
MUSLIM
teenager's
handbook

by Dilara Hafiz, Imran Hafiz, and Yasmine Hafiz

ginee seo books

Atheneum Books for Young Readers

New York   London   Toronto   Sydney

Atheneum Books for Young Readers

An imprint of Simon & Schuster Children's Publishing Division
1230 Avenue of the Americas, New York, New York 10020

Book design by Debra Sfetsios
The text for this book is set in Bauer Bodoni BT.
Manufactured in the United States of America
First Atheneum Books for Young Readers paperback edition
February 2009
10 9 8 7 6 5 4 3 2 1
CIP data for this book is available from the Library of Congress.
ISBN-13: 978-1-4169-8578-5
ISBN-10: 1-4169-8578-6
A previous edition of this title was previously published by Acacia
Publishing.

This book is dedicated to all the teenagers
out there who are searching. . . .
Don't give up on your dreams and ideals,
and may your spirituality guide you
to find inner peace
and happiness.

contents

A Note From Imam Feisal Abdul Rauf and Daisy Khan

Religion can be tough for teenagers. It's not easy to wake up earlier than your friends at school to pray, and it's even harder to refuse sausage at a baseball game because it's not *halal*. The differences between what our religion tells us to do and what others do around us can lead to hard decisions. And Muslim kids, without the help of good information about their religion, will sometimes choose the easier—rather than the more fulfilling and ultimately, better—way.

This book will help Muslim teenagers make these complicated and important choices. The genius of *The American Muslim Teenager's Handbook* is that it doesn't pretend that these decisions don't exist, or that they're not difficult for Muslim kids growing up in America today. Instead, it starts with the assumption that teenagers need help choosing, and it provides them with accessible information that can help guide their decisions.

All parents see themselves in the role of guiding their children's choices by teaching them about their faith. This represents the traditional format for passing on religious identity within any community. Although parent-led education is tried, true, and irreplaceable, American Muslim youth are showing more and more through their decisions that the generational disconnect—or "differences in expectations" between parents and children, as this book's authors call it—can make the knowledge and wisdom they gain from their parents difficult to swallow. This situation requires a go-between that can fill in this generational gap and teach children what they need to hear from eye level. This book functions as precisely that "friend" from who each child will learn successfully and excitedly consult as they make important decisions on a daily basis.

This book will serve as a wonderful tool for bridging the gap between young American Muslims and previous generations. It represents a uniquely Muslim *and* uniquely American effort, a testament to our faith's remarkable ability to develop itself with every new society to which it spreads. It functions as an invaluable tool in the hands of our community's future leaders, those who will carry this process forward until we can say that Islam has truly revitalized itself in our wonderful country. In addition, its refreshing perspective on religion as a whole is something that all Americans—Muslim as well as non-Muslim—can take to heart.

To the readers of this book, we say: You are the next generation. The challenges will be great, no doubt. But so will the successes. For the non-Muslims, we encourage each of you to learn from this important guide to Islam and become ambassadors for proper understanding and tolerance. For Muslim readers, this book will supplement the wisdom you gain from home and the mosque; study it along with other religious texts. With a firm grounding in your faith, you will enter the world as a confident Muslim *and* American man or woman.

The American Muslim Teenager's Handbook was deservedly awarded the 2008 Arizona Book Award for Best Book, Young Adult-Nonfiction. No surprise, it has been featured on Voice of America, and has been covered in newspapers from *The Guardian* in England to *The National* in Abu Dhabi. We proudly support this effort of a young man and woman taking a proactive and lead role in inspiring pride and serving as role models for Muslim teenagers.

—Imam Feisal Abdul Rauf, author of
What's Right With Islam Is What's Right With America, and Daisy Khan, executive director of
the American Society for Muslim Advancement

Foreword to the New Edition
by Professor Akbar Ahmed

Ever since James Dean forced the world to confront the problems of youth in *Rebel Without a Cause*, teenagers have had the spotlight on them. The teenage years are a time of challenge and turmoil for any young person. For Muslims, these years pose special challenges if they are living in the West. After 9/11, the challenge for the Muslim community grew exponentially as the media and ignorant commentators depicted Muslims as terrorist sympathizers and a fifth-column. While books were written for an older readership by older writers, there was little available for the young. *The American Muslim Teenager's Handbook* fills the vacuum admirably. Based on questionnaires that were sent out to one hundred and fifty high schoolers across the country, the book gives us a rare glimpse of how young Muslims think and act in the United States. Perhaps what distinguishes this book from other books is the fact that it captures the youthful vibrancy of its subject. There is a certain joy and optimism in the material.

I particularly appreciated two chapters in the book, which will give Muslims a sense of confidence and clarity. Chapter 14, "Inventions From the Muslim World: Where Did Algebra Come From, Anyway?," underlines the great contributions Muslims have made to world civilizations. Chapter 10, "The Four *D*s: Dating, Dancing, Drinking, and Drugs," tackles some of the social challenges facing Muslim Americans.

This book will help the young understand the daily challenges they face because it provides a clear "Muslim compass." The themes are that we are comfortable being proud Americans and being proud Muslims, and that we brought to these shores a rich and varied culture. Anyone wishing to learn about Islam—and

Muslims—especially those living in the West, should be grateful for this book.

As the father of a teenager, I am personally grateful to the authors, the Hafiz family, for this marvelous book. Not only has it provided me insights, but I also have enjoyed the freshness of its approach and style. The optimism, irony, and humor came as a breath of fresh air after the gloom of other writings about Islam. It is little wonder that the authors have been recognized widely—from the White House to the *New York Times*. May this book's voyage of enlightenment continue far and wide.

—Professor Akbar Ahmed, chair of
Islamic Studies, American University,
Washington, DC

Why You Should Read This Book
by Asma Gull Hasan

"Handbook." The word reminds you of the Boy Scouts or some other technical, outdoor-type venture. A handbook is meant to be a kind of manual or guide to a new place or adventure. So why a handbook for American Muslim teens? Because the book you are holding is meant to do that as well. Think of it as a travel guide for a young American Muslim. Which direction should you go in? What street should you take? This handbook can't make your decisions for you, but it can give you the tools every young Muslim—actually, every person—needs to make those decisions for yourself. In navigating through the wilds of American culture, balancing it with one's Islamic faith and ethnic heritage, one surely needs a handbook just as much as the Boy Scouts do—maybe more so!

I wish this book had existed when I was a teenager. Instead, I had to figure out the message myself, which I did. But I want better for you, reader. I want you to be able to do more, accomplish more, and achieve more than I or the members of my generation have. To do this, you will need to know what this book contains. The most important lesson to learn is that your Islam is *yours*, not anyone else's—not your parents', your siblings', or that whacky uncle who lectures you on the Quran at every Eid. Be patient with yourself. No one becomes a perfect Muslim overnight. It's a lifelong journey. Even the Prophet Muhammad did not learn of Islam until he was past forty years old. Do the best you can, and always keep trying.

Now, I know parents might be a little reluctant. It's certainly difficult to turn your teen loose into the wilderness. That is *not* what this book is advocating. This book was written by two teens and their parent. They discussed the topics that went into the book— both typical and controversial. Their relationship is much stronger for it. Would you rather have your children learn about these things from neighborhood kids? Or would you like them to learn at their own pace, at home, and encouraged by their "handbook" to discuss their questions with you?

There's no magic formula to being a successful teen, but this book comes close to it. Focus on the chapters that interest you most, and reread them as you need more guidance. Read what other kids your age had to say about the same things, and use this book as a springboard to discuss these issues with your parents and friends. Good luck!

—Asma Gull Hasan, author of *American Muslims: The New Generation* and *Why I Am a Muslim: An American Odyssey*

Why We Wrote This Book

The idea for this book began innocently enough. My daughter and I were in a bookstore a few years ago. I wandered past the bargain books section while she made a beeline for the young adult/teen section. After browsing, selecting a few books, and making our purchases, she remarked to me, "Mom, why aren't there any books for Muslim teenagers? I saw some interesting ones for Christian teens. I wish there was one for Muslim teens too." I didn't have a good answer for her. A few weeks later, my son related an incident in his middle school when a group of kids labeled him as a member of the Taliban. Despite assertions to the contrary, he was unable to convince them, as they were certain that all Muslims believed in an extremist version of Islam. His frustration was palpable as he remarked to me, "I wish there was something I could give them that would basically explain Islam to them. Not a boring textbook, but something interesting!"

As a mother of two teenagers, I know from personal experience that young adults are full of curiosity and are inclined to ask "Why?" before doing what they're told. As a Muslim in America, I also realize the unique challenges and opportunities facing these teens. In a way, Muslim teenagers are poised to enjoy the best of all possible worlds. They are free to practice their religion in a multi-religious country. They can also tap into the rich cultural heritage of their ancestors by joining international clubs, learning to speak different languages, and enjoying the cultural diversity that defines America. But too often Muslim teens are confused or ignorant about their own religion, whether by choice or lack of opportunity.

This handbook seeks to stimulate and educate, but in no way purports to be a definitive guide to Islam. The study of any religion can require a lifetime of dedication—Islam is a religion that is more than fourteen hundred years old. While countless scholars have studied and defined the myriad facets of Islam, I have chosen to address the specific topic of Muslim teenagers in America from the perspective of Muslim teens themselves. By choosing such a specific but often overlooked audience, my teenagers and I are hoping to grab the attention of a section of American Muslims by engaging them in a dialogue of teen issues and concerns.

Too often Muslims portray Islam in negatives such as "You can't do this" or "You can't do that." The religion can seem loaded down with so much stereotypical cultural baggage that it's no wonder that young Muslims feel like it's an overwhelming burden. We need to lighten up! By encouraging discussion, we'd like to invite readers to examine what aspects of their religion are truly requirements of the faith. Think about Islam as a "can do" religion. Following the basic rules of any religion should still allow you plenty of room to have fun and enjoy life in a morally correct manner—It all depends on your perspective!

I strongly encourage any reader to further their education by reading more books about Islam, or better yet, pick up the Quran and study it. My children and I have written this book with the best of intentions—to let Muslim teenagers know that they are not alone or forgotten. God willing, anyone who picks up this book will bene-fit from a little of the wisdom and truth that is quoted by teenagers from all walks of life.

—Dilara Hafiz,
Paradise Valley, Valley

How to Use This Book

How many times have you heard your parents say "Why can't you be more like ___?" (Fill in the blank with either "your sister," "your cousin," or "Mrs. So and So's son") Or the ever popular "When are you going to grow up?" Being a teenager is exciting, challenging, and, at times, confusing, but growing up as a Muslim teenager in America can seem an even more overwhelming task. Where do you go for answers? To whom can you turn for advice? Even though your parents, teachers, and friends are all sensible choices, sometimes the topics seem too important to trust to impromptu discussions.

Religion is just one of those topics: serious, important, maybe even "uncool," but also essential to the spiritual well-being of any God-conscious person. Teenagers and *religion*? At first glance, maybe these two concepts don't seem to fit together at all. But who needs factual, down-to-earth advice more than an American Muslim teenager facing peer pressure, hormonal mood swings (pimples included, free of charge!), and the demands of an ever-changing society? While several excellent books offering guidance to parents of teenagers are currently on the market, there is a dearth of information written by teens, for teens, and most important, in an easy-to-read, teen-friendly format. Have a question about prayer? Turn to Chapter 3 and check out the "How to Pray" section. Confused about the etiquette of fasting? Chapter 5 will fill in the gaps in your knowledge while keeping your mind off your hunger pangs. The results of the American Muslim teenagers' questionnaire will surprise you—and hopefully not bore you—and possibly encourage you to learn more about Islam and other faiths.

Whether you're an experienced Muslim, new to religion in general, or just curious about Muslim beliefs, this book will provoke you. Keep an open mind and an open heart, for God loves those who search for knowledge. Islam is the fastest-growing yet the most misunderstood religion in America. By answering some basic questions and reviewing widespread Islamic beliefs, this handbook will equip Muslim teens in America with self-confidence to face the post-9/11 world they find themselves in, as well as initiate an interfaith dialogue with like-minded readers. So go ahead and find a topic that interests you and read on!

A Note to the Reader

Throughout this book, we have used quotations from Ahmed Ali's 1984 translation of the Quran, which is published by Princeton University Press, as well as Abdullah Yusuf Ali's 2001 edition of the Quran, which is published by Tahrike Tarsile Qur'an, Inc., Elmhurst, New York.

In the spring of 2002, we mailed out *The American Muslim Teenager's Handbook* questionnaire to more than forty full-time and part-time Islamic schools in the United States. The results from approximately one hundred and fifty respondents are included throughout the book, under the heading "What Do Teens *Really* Think?" We'd like to thank the following schools for participating: Al Hedayah Academy, Ft. Worth, Texas; College Prepatory School of America, Lombard, Illinois; Islamic Foundation School, Villa Park, Illinois at the Islamic Center of Columbus, Columbus, Ohio; and Islamic Weekend School at the Islamic Center of the Northeast Valley, Scottsdale, Arizona.

Islam

101

An Overview of the Beginning

> "All those who believe,
> and the Jews and the Sabians and the Christians,
> in fact, any one who believes in God and the Last Day,
> and performs good deeds,
> Will have nothing to fear or regret."
> —Quran, 5:69

*I*slam is the name given to the message revealed by the Prophet Muhammad in AD 610 in Mecca, a small city in Arabia. He continued to receive revelations from God, transmitted by the Angel Gabriel during the next twenty-three years. The word "Islam" literally means "submission" or "peace," and in the context of religion, it is commonly defined as "one who finds peace through submission to God." Islam is the second largest religion in the world after Christianity, with more than 1.3 billion followers. Muslims come from many different ethnic backgrounds, bringing with them varying customs, languages, and cultural nuances when practicing their common faith. Thus, Islam in action is a colorful and fluid tapestry made up of interesting people from all walks of life, sharing common beliefs and common values. In reality, there is no such thing as an "average Muslim." For example, your Muslim neighbor is just as likely to come from Bangkok, Thailand, as he is from Boise, Idaho!

Why did Islam originate in the Middle East, six centuries after Christianity? Muslims believe that God has been sending us the same essential message since the days of Adam and Eve. He has been asking us to believe in Him, worship only Him, and live righteously on Earth in the knowledge that we will someday return to Him. Pretty simple message, right? So how and when did we go astray? Why are there so many different religions when many of them have so much in common? Well, for a start, God rarely gave His instructions in writing, but because we need guidance for the littlest things in life, so it makes sense that we need the instructions for life in writing. Maybe if Adam had had a handy little pocket guide to refer to in times of doubt, he and Eve would have ignored Satan's whispers of temptation, which encouraged them to sample fruit from the one tree in the Garden that God had forbidden to them. However, it's not appropriate to second-guess God. He eventually gave His game plan in writing, in the form of the Sacred Scrolls, to Abraham, arguably the first monotheist, who shunned the worship of idols.

Abraham lived about four thousand years ago (1800 BC) in the Mesopotamian Valley. His father was a maker of the idols and statues that the people of the community worshipped. Abraham, however, questioned his people's beliefs and attempted to show them the futility of worshipping idols. He further demonstrated through analogy that it is foolish to worship a star, the moon, or the sun, as all these Heavenly objects disappear from sight during various times of a twenty-four-hour day. It was an incredible leap of faith for him to convince his community to place their faith in the worship of an unseen God. However, after much trials and even ostracism, the strength of Abraham's conviction managed to sway the majority of his peers. Muslims believe that in the ensuing years, Abraham and his son Ishmael rebuilt the Kaabah in Mecca, Saudi Arabia, the first building dedicated to the worship of the one God that was originally built by Adam.

Thus Abraham is viewed in a religious context as the first mono-theist and the patriarch of Judaism, Christianity, and Islam. These three "Abrahamic" faiths, as they have come to be known, can all trace their roots back to Abraham. His story is described in the Old Testament as well as in the Quran. Muslims trace their ancestry back to Abraham through his

son Ishmael, while Jews trace their lineage back to him through his second son Isaac. The similarities in Abraham's message, when viewed through the individual lenses of these three religions, is remarkable; confirming Abraham as their common ancestor emphasizes to Muslims the belief that God has been sending the same message to mankind, yet man himself forgets or changes His words.

Muslims accept the notion that God selected various people throughout history to receive His message in written form. In Islam, these prophets are referred to as "messengers."

In addition to these messengers, God chose numerous men as His prophets, to teach the people how to grow closer to God through living a righteous life on Earth. Countless prophets from the Old Testament also appear in the Quran, including Adam, Noah, Jacob, Solomon, Jonah, and Aaron, to name a few. Hence the body of historical fables is strikingly similar in all three religions, and Muslims revere all these prophets and their received books as divinely inspired by God. How and when did Islam originate if God had already revealed His message to mankind several times in the past? Although Judaism and Christianity were quite widespread by the sixth century, Muslims believe that their practice had begun to differ from

Messenger	Book
Abraham/Ibrahim	Scrolls
Moses/Musa	Torah
Jesus/Issa	Gospel
David/Dawud	Psalms
Muhammad	Quran

the initial message at this time, perhaps as a result of political and social influences from the surrounding communities. Thus it was necessary for God to resend the same message through a different messenger, this time in writing and in Arabic, so that the Arab people could understand it for themselves.

Muslims believe that the message of the Quran is a basic one for all humanity, therefore numerous translations of the Quran exist throughout the world. Previous messages had been revealed in both Hebrew or Aramaic—languages that had changed significantly throughout the years, resulting in discrepancies creeping into the numerous translations at that time.

Islam recognized Muhammad as the last chosen messenger in the year AD 610. Muhammad was a pious man who was distressed at the rampant materialism and inequalities he observed in Meccan society around him. His contemplative nature led him to retreat periodically to a cave in the nearby mountains to meditate on the meaning and purpose of life. It was during one such retreat that the Angel Gabriel appeared to him and instructed him to "Read." Thus began a series of revelations that continued for the next twenty-three years. Muslims believe that Muhammad is the "Seal of the Prophets," which means that God no longer needs to send another messenger at this time. His message is contained in a written form—the Quran. The essential message remains the same: to believe in the one God, to worship Him, and to do as many good deeds as possible in order to be reunited with God in the hereafter.

Besides the twenty-two Arab countries, there are another

thirty-five countries with Muslim-majority populations. This total of fifty-seven countries represents about one-third of the total 191 independent countries in the world.

Fundamentally, Judaism, Christianity, and Islam have far more in common with one another than any of the other world religions, such as Hinduism, Buddhism, or Sikhism. Ultimately, all religions are a road map to life. Whether we choose to stay on that path or to explore side roads is entirely up to us, but we may be pleasantly surprised to learn that we all end up at the same destination.

Children of Abraham

Judaism	Christianity	Islam
1800 BC/Abraham	AD 27/Jesus	AD 610/Muhammad
Belief in God	Belief in God as part of Holy Trinity	Belief in God
Torah (Hebrew Bible)	Bible	Quran
One earthly life	One earthly life	One earthly life
Day of Judgment	Day of Judgment	Day of Judgment
15 million followers	2.1 billion followers	1.3 billion followers

You've probably heard people refer to "the five pillars of Islam." Do they summarize the faith? Most Muslims are taught the five pillars (see p. 7) at an early age, but once they begin reading the Quran, they're often surprised to learn about the other aspects of their religion. In addition to these pillars, which focus on the outward signs of the faith, there are five articles of faith, which are more Abrahamic in nature in that they emphasize the continuity of Islam's message (see the box on the right). The essential

The Five Articles of Faith

1. Belief in God
2. Belief in His angels
3. Belief in His books (Scrolls, Torah, Psalms, Gospel, Quran)
4. Belief in His prophets
5. Belief in the Day of Judgment

message of kindness, goodness, and righteousness is evident on each page of the Quran. Focusing on the belief in the one God and performing as many good deeds as possible are two vital elements repeated the most often in the Quran. There are varying degrees of observance of the five pillars in any Muslim society, and American Muslims are no different from any other faith group in their variety. So don't judge everyone you meet in accordance to your standards or understanding of their religion—sometimes outward appearances can be deceptive. Millions of people of all faiths are good people who practice love, charity, and community service without their neighbors being aware of their actions!

The Five Pillars of Islam

1. Declaration of Faith (Shahadah)
2. Prayer (Salat)
3. Charity (Zakat)
4. Fasting (Sawm/Ramadan)
5. Hajj (Pilgrimage to Mecca)

Shaha

dah: Islam's Central Belief

"There is no compulsion in matter of faith.
Distinct is the way of guidance now from error.
He who turns away from the forces of evil
and believes in God, will surely hold fast
to a handle that is strong and unbreakable,
for God hears all and knows everything."
—Quran, 2:256

hat does it mean to be a Muslim? Ask ten people and you'll probably receive ten different answers. The standard criteria for being Muslim is to be "one who submits to the will of God." In plain English, that translates to "believing in God." Most Muslims would say that uttering the *Shahadah* (also known as the Profession of Faith, or the Islamic Creed) at least once in one's life qualifies a person to call himself a Muslim. Following is a transliteration of the *Shahadah* and an English translation:

I bear witness that there is no god but God, and
that Muhammad is His Messenger.

The emphatic assertion that there is only one God serves to highlight this most central belief of Islam; that, indeed, the declarative "no god but God" rules out the belief in idols or a pantheon of gods, such as in the early Roman and Greek fundamentals of mythology. The statement also includes the fact that Muhammad, while being the last Prophet, was only a messenger and a man, not a divine entity in and of himself. This belief that Muhammad was a human being, born from the flesh of a man and a woman, who was capable of error and human weakness, also instructs Muslims that no one is perfect. Only God is all-knowing, divine, and perfect.

The *Shahadah* is beautiful in its simplicity, but being a Muslim involves more than reciting this phrase once in a lifetime or only on Fridays or even seventeen times a day. Being a Muslim is a way of life. By promising to "bear witness," you are declaring you will live your life with the belief that God sees your every action, knows your innermost thoughts, and is ever present in your life. This state of *taqwa*, or "God-consciousness," greatly simplifies your life as you now have a guide (God), with the Quran as your road map. Or in other words, when in doubt, do the right thing.

Trusting that God is in your life will enable you to be more confident, more observant, and more humble—a unique combination that many people, both Muslims and non-Muslims, constantly aspire to but few actually achieve. The foundation of the Judeo-Christian-Islamic belief system is the belief in the one God. All three religions refer to the same God, which may surprise some people.

Why Are _You_ A Muslim?

50%—Because my parents are.

20%—Because of my beliefs/Because I believe in the teachings of Islam.

15%—Because it's cool—Muslims rock!

15%—Because the more I learn about it, the more I realize that I really am a Muslim.

The Inside Scoop:
What Do Teens _Really_ Think?

Arooj, age 14, Ohio: "Truthfully, I started out as a Muslim by name, which I got from my parents, but over time I realized Islam was really what's right for me and that is when I believe I became a Muslim by heart and not simply by name."

Maymuna, age 11, Texas: "Because I understand Islam and it's so clear."

Faraz, age 15, Ohio: "I was born a Muslim, so I have an advantage, because I have been taught Islam while having an open mind. I am a Muslim because this religion makes sense, while having logical guidelines."

Liza, age 16, Illinois: "I was Christian, then I converted when I felt the time was right. That was when my heart was in it. I am a Muslim because I want to be. I feel that it is the only religion that truly serves Allah."

Amira, age 16, Ohio (Thank you, Ohio, for all your responses!): "This is a difficult question. I was born a Muslim, but did not fully embrace Islam until I was fourteen and a half years old. I was a sophomore in high school, and at the beginning of the year I was still wearing short skirts and T-shirts. Something happened to make me realize that I was doing something wrong, and I started being more modest and praying five times daily. My parents never forced me to become a Muslim. They let me realize it on my own, and I love them for that.

Julia, age 12, Arizona: "Because of the beliefs and what the religion is all about."

How **Strong** Is Your Faith?

1. Your geography teacher mistakenly identifies Mecca as a city in Iraq. You:

    a) Slide lower in your chair and pretend to be fascinated by the interior of your desk.

    b) Tentatively whisper to your neighbor, "I think he means it's in Saudi Arabia—or somewhere over there."

    c) Frantically wave your hand in the air to correct the error.

2. Your whole class is excitedly preparing for the annual Christmas play. You:

    a) Pretend you have a doctor's appointment during rehearsals—every Tuesday and Thursday afternoon for the next two months!

    b) Explain to your teacher that, as a Muslim, you

don't feel comfortable being an actor, you'd be happy to help out with costumes or set design instead.

c) Try out for the part of the camel (either front half or back half) and hope that your parents won't recognize you beneath all that fake fur.

3. Everyone is excited about attending the prom, but you're not allowed to go as it requires a date. You:

a) Loudly protest about the amount of time and money that is commonly spent on prom preparations.

b) Realize that this event is important to your friends, so you offer to help with decorations and setting up, then spend the evening at home with your family.

c) Politely refuse to accept any dates and explain that in Islam, physical contact between unmarried people (such as slow dancing) is frowned upon, but try and get a group of friends to go together "as friends."

4. You went to the morning prayers on Eid, so you're late to school. Everyone asks, "Where were you?" You:

a) Tell them you had a dentist appointment (and pretend your cheeks are numb with novocaine).

b) Proudly declare to the class, "I was at Eid

prayers!,'" then explain that holiday's significance
in your religion.

    c) Pretend you've temporarily gone deaf!

**5. Your school is preparing for an interfaith assembly and
asks for volunteers to speak onstage about their religion/
beliefs. You:**

    a) Ignore the announcement and hope no one
       volunteers you.

    b) Take charge of the event and delegate random

people to research and present a variety of different religions.

c) Volunteer to explain your beliefs in an interesting and informative manner.

6. You overhear a group of ignorant bullies harassing some other Muslim students who are fasting during Ramadan. You:

a) Ask your principal to make an announcement over the PA explaining Ramadan.

b) Tell the bullies that they should try fasting to lose some of the unnecessary fat that is clogging up their brains—then run!

c) Pretend the rules of Ramadan don't apply to you while you chow down in the cafeteria with your friends.

Answers

1. At least *b*, but *c* if you're brave enough. It's not easy correcting the teacher, but world geography is important.

2. *B*, although *c* would be pretty funny. There's nothing wrong with participating in celebrating someone else's religion from an interfaith point of view. It doesn't mean that you accept or believe in it, so if you enjoy acting, go right ahead.

3. Definitely not *a*—you'll unnecessarily alienate your friends. Either *b* or *c* should be fine if you first clear it with your parents.

4. *B*, because it's the truth, plus *a* would be an embarrassment during lunch, because you'd have to dribble your drink out of one side of your mouth to keep up the dentist story!

5. *C* is preferable, but *b* would be okay too since it would be a way for everyone to learn something about a different religion by actually researching it rather than just listening to someone speak about it.

6. Only choose *b* if you're on the track team, otherwise *a* is the way to go.

Chapter 3

Prayer:

All Your Prayers Answered

> "Your only friends are God and His Messenger,
> and those who believe and are steadfast in devotion,
> who pay zakat and bow in homage (before God)."
> —Quran, 5:55

he most important belief in Islam is the belief in the one God. (By the way, "Allah" means "God" in Arabic; not a Muslim god or an Arab god, just "God"). Allah is God—the same God worshipped by Jews and Christians all over the world. Monotheism, the belief in one God, is the central tenet of all three Abrahamic faiths—namely, Judaism, Christianity, and Islam. They're referred to as Abrahamic because they all look to Abraham as the first person who worshipped one God. Traditionally, Muslims include Adam as the first prophet in a long line of prophets. Abraham is recognized for his role in turning away from polytheism to monotheism, therefore his name has been conferred upon the three main monotheistic faiths.

So that there is no confusion in anyone's mind, God will be referred to as "God" from now on, since this book is in English. (If it were translated into Arabic, "Allah" would be the word of choice, just as "Dieu" would be selected for the French translation or "Dios" for the Spanish translation.)

The Quran has several themes that are repeated throughout its pages. The most obvious one is the belief in God. On almost every page, God is asking us to believe in Him, to worship only Him, and to have faith in Him. Assuming no one has a problem with believing in God, let's move on to another important theme: prayer. God continually reminds us to pray, but He doesn't need our prayers, does He? Why should we pray to someone we can't see or get a response from? Good questions—Now let's search for some answers.

What is prayer? Prayer is talking to God. In Islam, prayer most often refers to the five required daily prayers that consists of *rakas*, or units of prayer. The prayer is memorized and recited in Arabic. However, you can recite a prayer or supplication whenever you feel like it, in whatever language you feel comfortable with (probably English!), and wherever you happen to be—sitting in the car, in class before a test, or before you begin a meal.

Do I have to pray? No one can force you to pray. Remember, there is no compulsion in religion, but if you believe that God wants you to pray, you will. Don't pray if you're doing it out of guilt or fear or parental pressure. Pray because you truly want to.

Am I still a Muslim if I don't pray? Yes, of course. Being a Muslim is a state of mind, and no one knows what's in your heart other than you and God. Don't pray to impress others—do it for God.

I don't know how to pray—Help! No problem! Open to the handy "How to Pray" section on pp. 25–31, and keep the book on the floor in front of you as you pray. Pretty soon you'll have the basics memorized and will be praying like a pro.

Does each prayer of the day have a special name? Yes, the names of the prayers, in order, are Fajr, Zuhr, Asr, Maghrib, and Isha.

Five Reasons to Pray

1. God asks us to.

2. Parents tell us to—but they need to first teach us how to!

3. We should give thanks for our blessings.

4. It makes us feel better inside (not the "hot chocolate with mini-marshmallows on a cold day" feeling, but the "I found twenty dollars and turned it in to the lost and found" feeling).

5. It's the right thing to do.

6. It can't make your life any worse, but it may make your life a lot better.

Yes, there are six reasons listed, not five, but then you can probably think of many more. . . .

See, this prayer thing may be easier than it seems.

Do Teens Really Pray? *Honestly?*

Samiah, age 11, Arizona: "I do pray every Maghrib prayer in the month of Ramadan and when we go to special prayers for funerals. I don't pray five times a day all the time, because I haven't memorized some parts, but I plan to memorize them soon."

Sumbul, age 14, Illinois: "It's really weird. I have months when I seriously won't miss a single prayer. And then there will be times when I'll miss two or three prayers all together. Isha and Fajr are the hardest, but I feel the best after praying them."

Anonymous, age 14: "Yes, I miss a few daily . . . only because I am so lazy . . . but I try and make them up."

Bashirah, age 15, Illinois: "Yes, I do pray. I usually pray only three out of the five prayers, because for some reason it no longer feels as holy or spiritual. It's feeling more like a chore and sometimes I get mad at Allah for not being there like He said He would if you're a true believer and pray, etc. So I guess I don't believe in it as much. But I pray three times a day just in case He does."

Anonymous, age 16: "I will not lie—not regularly. I know it's wrong and that I should be praying, but my laziness takes over. I'm trying to improve on that."

Amira, age 16, Ohio: "Yes, I do pray a minimum of five times a day. If I'm feeling particularly happy or sad that day, I'll do extra."

Reyhan, age 16, Ohio: "I pray five times a day because it says in the Quran that you should be steadfast in prayer. I believe that if you are not steadfast in your prayer, you will forget Allah."

Lots of Anonymous, all ages, all states: "No, I don't know how" or "No, I don't know why not."

Although the Quran does not specify the actual prayer times, there are numerous references in which God asks us to bow in worship to Him: before sunrise, after sunset, in the middle of the night, when the sun is at its peak, and during the sun's decline "from the meridian to the darkening of the night" (Quran, 17:78). Thus, Muslims follow these instructions to the best of their abilities, emulating the manner in which the Prophet Muhammad taught his early followers to pray. It would be a fallacy to assume that each and every Muslim observes the obligatory five prayers, however, it is important to remember the reason behind the emphasis on regular, daily prayer: Formulating good habits can keep you focused on your life's goals and instill obedience as well as give structure to your daily life. Just like yoga is a physical discipline for the body, prayer is a mental discipline for the soul. It's important to enjoy the time-out from the daily grind that prayer can provide. An overwhelming majority of Muslims agree that the five daily prayers are an undisputable requirement—whether they fulfill this requirement or not. Obviously the Quran is beseeching all believers in God to pray as often as possible for their own well-being and peace of mind, but each of us is an individual on his or her own spiritual journey. Only God can judge the sincerity of our prayers. There is no official clergy or priesthood in Islam. Rather, the emphasis is on a direct connection between the individual and God. So whether you're a newcomer to prayer or a five-times-a-day prayer achiever, there's always room to improve both quality and quantity in your prayers. Never give up!

How to Pray:
A Step-by-Step Guide

1. Perform *wudu*, a cleansing ritual. Basically, it's washing your hands, face, arms, and legs. (Check the prayer glossary on p. 32 for an explanation.)

2. Stand upright on a clean surface (or a rug) and face the direction of the Kaabah (Qiblah). See the prayer glossary on p. 33 for an explanation.)

3. Say your intention, or *niyah*. (See the glossary on p. 33 for details. And no, you're not allowed to just skip this part and read the definitions . . . Well, okay, you can glance at the prayer glossary if it helps.)

4. Raise your hands to your ears and say *"Allahu Akbar"* ("God is Great").

5. Cross your hands in front of your chest and recite the Surah al-Fatihah, (The Opening) in Arabic as follows:

> *Bismillahir rahmanir rahim.*
> *Al hamdu lil lahi rabbil alamin.*
> *Arrahmanir rahim*
> *Maliki yawmiddin.*
> *Iyyaka na'budu wa iyyaka nasta'in.*
> *Ihdinas siratal mustaqim.*
> *Siratal ladhina an 'amta 'alaihim,*
> *Ghairil maghdubi alaihim*
> *Wa lad dallin.*
> *Ameen. (1:1–7)*

Translation:

> In the name of God, most benevolent, ever-merciful.
> All praise be to God, Lord of all the worlds,
> Most beneficent, ever-merciful,
> King of the Day of Judgment.

You alone we worship, and to You alone we turn for help.

Guide us (O Lord) to the path that is straight,

The path of those You have blessed,

Not of those who have earned Your anger,

nor those who have gone astray.

Amen.

6. Recite another surah from the Quran. For example, Surah al-Ikhlas (Purity):

Qul hu wal lahu ahad,
Allahus samad,
Lam yalid wa lam yulad,
Wa lam ya kul lahu kufuwan ahad.
  (112:1–4)

Translation:

He is God, the one the most
  unique,
God, the immanently [*sic*]
  indispensable.
He has begotten no one,
and is begotten of none.
There is no one comparable to
  Him.

7. Bend down from the waist (*ruku*), saying, *"Allahu Akbar"* ("God is Great"), place your hands on your knees and say *"Subhana Rabbiyal Azim"* ("Glory to my Lord, the Great") three times.

8. Stand up from the bowing position and say *"Sami Allahu liman hamidah. Rabbana wa lakal hamd."* ("God hears those who praise Him. Our Lord, praise be to You.") This standing position is called *"qiyam."*

9. Say *"Allahu Akbar"* ("God is Great") while kneeling upon the floor with your knees, forehead, nose, and palms touching the floor. (This is called "prostrating.") Recite *"Subhana Rabbiyal A'la"* ("Glory to my Lord, the Highest") three times.

This prostrating position is called *"sajdah."*

10. Sit on your knees, with your palms placed on them while saying, *"Allahu Akbar"* ("God is Great"). Rest a moment. This short pause

between the two prostrations is called *"jalsah."*

11. Prostrate upon the floor again, repeating, *"Subhana Rabbiyal A'la"* ("Glory to my Lord, the Highest") three times.

12. Get up while saying, *"Allahu Akbar"* ("God is Great"). This completes one *raka*. The second *raka* is similar to the first, except a different surah is recited after the recitation of Surah al-Fatihah.

13. Following the second prostration, a longer *jalsah* is performed while repeating the following prayer, called "At-Tashahhud":

At-tahiyyatu li-Llahi
Wa-s-salawatu wat-tayyibatu
Assalamu 'alai-ka 'ayyuhu-n-nabiyyu
Wa rahamtu-lahi wa barakatu-Hu
Assalamu 'alaina
Wa 'ala ibadilLahi-s-salihin
'Ashhadu 'an la illaha 'illa-Llahu
Wa 'ashhadu 'anna Muhammadan
'Abdu-Hu wa rasulu-Hu. (Hadith)

Translation:

All prayer is for God
And worship and goodness
Peace be on you, O Prophet
And the mercy of God and His blessings
Peace be on us
And on the righteous servants of God
I bear witness that there is no God but God
And that Muhammad is His servant and messenger.

Note that when you recite the "Ashhadu 'an la" section of the prayer, you raise your right index finger up from your knee in symbolic remembrance of the one God.

14. After the At-Tashahhud, you recite an additional prayer called "*salawat*," which confers blessings on the prophets, particularly Muhammad and Abraham. The *salawat* is as follows:

Allahumma salli 'ala Muhammadin
Wa 'ala 'ali Muhammadin
Kama sallaita 'ala 'Ibrahima
Wa 'ala 'ali 'Ibrahima,
'Inna-Ka Hamidun Majid
'Allahumma barik 'ala Muhammadin
Wa 'ala 'ali Muhammadin

Kama barakta 'ala 'Ibrahima

Wa 'ala 'ali 'Ibrahima,

'Inna-Ka Hamidun Majid. (Hadith)

Translation:

O God, greetings upon Muhammad

And the family of Muhammad

As You greeted Abraham

And the family of Abraham.

Indeed! You are the Praiseworthy and Glorious One.

O God, bless Muhammad

And the family of Muhammad

As You blessed Abraham

And the family of Abraham.

Indeed! You are the Praiseworthy and Glorious One.

15. After saying these prayers, you face toward the right and say, "*Assalamu alaikum wa rahmatullah*" ("Peace and mercy of God be upon you"), and then face toward the left and repeat the same words.

Congratulations! You've just completed two *raka*s of prayers! Not to confuse you, but each of the five required daily prayers has a different number of *raka*s that is customarily performed with each one. For a prayer that is longer than two *raka*s, the At-Tashahhud is recited only after the second *raka*. Then you would repeat another *raka*, recite only the Surah al-Fatihah, then complete the *raka* as instructed above. It sounds complicated, but really isn't that difficult, especially if you pray alongside someone who knows what he or she is doing. Check the Internet for a mosque near you, or call the closest university or college. There's sure to be a group of Muslims who get together to pray, especially on Fridays. (Friday is the day of congregational prayer in Islam.) Good luck!

Name	Time of Day	Number of Rakas
Fajr	Before sunrise	2
Zuhr	After 12:00 PM	4
Asr	Midafternoon	4
Maghrib	Immediately after sunset	3
Isha	Night	4

Prayer Glossary

du'as: Basically, prayers or supplications that can be uttered silently or out loud, in congregation or alone, at any time or place.

fard: obligatory, compulsory. This term refers to the five required daily prayers, which entail standing, bowing, and prostrating.

niyah: literally means "intention." By reiterating your intention to pray before each prayer, you are reminding yourself that you are consciously performing an act of worship to and for God, and not merely performing a ritual automatically, like a robot.

qiblah: the direction in which Muslims face while they say their prayers, which is facing the direction of the Kaabah in Mecca in Saudi Arabia. Muslims do not worship the Kaabah. Rather, Kaabah represents a spiritual focus for prayer since Muslims revere the Kaabah as the first house of worship that was dedicated to the one God.

Sunnah: the actions of Prophet Muhammad. Since Muslims view Prophet Muhammad as the one person who embodies the highest levels of piousness and righteousness, they aspire to emulate his personal habits in an attempt to improve themselves and bring themselves closer to God. Prophet Muhammad often performed additional prayers after the *fard* prayers were completed, thus many Muslims also habitually say these additional prayers in acknowledgment of his practice.

Wudu: a ritual cleansing before prayer. Specifically, the washing of your hands, mouth, nose, face, arms, head, ears, and feet. Symbolically representing the spiritual cleansing that occurs when you pray. If water is unavailable, you can use clean sand or earth.

Zakat:

Chapter 4

Charity—
What Does It *Really* Mean?

"If you give alms openly, it is well;
but if you do it secretly and give to the poor, that is better.
This will absolve you of some of your sins;
and God is cognizant of all you do."

—Quran, 2:271

n addition to faith and prayer, the Quran emphasizes the practice of doing good deeds. It's not enough to be a pious person in your head and live a life of excellent isolation. It's imperative to put your good intentions into practice and actually go out and *do good*. By translating good thoughts into good deeds, you "walk the talk." Sometimes it's boring and dull to always "be good" (aren't those the last words you always hear as you leave home? "Be good!") Well, try *doing* good for a change.

It's sometimes a challenge, but it's never dull or boring, and you may be surprised at all the good vibes you generate around you.

Islam emphasizes the importance of doing good deeds on a regular basis, which leads us to the topic of *zakat* (alms giving, or charity). Alms are things given to relieve poverty, or in order to help the poor. The concept of donating a portion of your savings or excess wealth on an annual basis is a sensible practice of welfare, especially in countries where the needy may not benefit from the existence of a welfare state. In addition, it's a small attempt to redistribute wealth in order to reduce the disparity between the haves and the have nots.

If a Muslim donates food, clothing, or money to the less fortunate around him, he is purifying his wealth in the sense that he can now enjoy his blessings with a clear conscience. By practicing charity on a regular basis, Muslims can truly appreciate what God has given them while reminding themselves that they may one day be in need of charity. This relationship between the rich and the poor is an important one because it serves as a reminder about the fleeting nature of material wealth. The recommended amount to donate is 2.5% of your net worth, but whether you choose to donate more or less is between you and God.

"But for those who believe and work deeds of righteousness—to them We shall give a Home in Heaven— an excellent reward for those who do good!"

—Quran, 29:58

A Teen's List
of Charitable Ideas

1. Donate old clothes on a regular basis.

Reward: Your closet is less cluttered.

2. Donate your favorite outfit instead of old stuff.

Reward: Imagine the look of happiness some lucky person will have!

3. Turn over a week's allowance to your broke friend.

Reward: Maybe she'll do the same for you one day.

4. Babysit for free.

Reward: Your parents will be surprised and impressed.

5. Treat the stranger behind you by paying his/her parking/ admission/coffee.

Reward: You'll put someone in a good mood for the rest of the day.

6. Drop twenty dollars instead of a dollar in the school fundraiser box.

Reward: The orphanage/homeless shelter/AIDS clinic has more money to help others.

7. Hand over your allowance to a homeless person.

Reward: You know you did a good deed, regardless of what they spend the money on.

8. Fine-tune a skill/talent and use it to do good. If you're in a band, play for free at a concert for charity.

Reward: People get to enjoy your talent (maybe they'll hire you for a gig!).

The More You Give, the More You Receive
(Seriously)

- Give a portion of your allowance to a charity.
- Give freely of your smile.
- Give generously around the house by cleaning up after yourself.
- Give up whining, complaining, and generally being a pain in the…neck.
- Give your brain power help to those in need (help your little brother with his homework!).
- Give a grateful word to your parents when they come home from work.
- Give up your Sunday afternoons to helping the elderly in your neighborhood with their chores, yard work, etc.
- Receive applause, appreciation, gratitude (okay, some disbelief, too!) from family, friends, and most important, God.

"Easy have we made the Qur'an to understand."

—Quran, 54:17

Chapter 5

It's Ramadan:
Tips for a Successful Fast

> "O believers, fasting is enjoined [prescribed] on you
> as it was on those before you,
> so that you might become righteous."
>
> —Quran, 2:183

hat does "enjoined" really mean? Have you ever wondered about that? According to *Merriam-Webster's* dictionary, "enjoin" means "to direct or impose by authoritative order . . ." Hmm . . . that helps . . . a little. "Prescribed" means "to lay down as a guide, direction, or rule of action, to designate or order the use of as a remedy." Now *that* makes more sense. God is commanding the believers to fast, as their ancestors had done in the past, for their own good. Just as a prescription for medicine is intended to cure your illness, fasting is prescribed as medicine to cure greed, lack of control, and by extension, teach spiritual fulfillment rather than physical fulfillment.

Think of fasting as shopping. You see this fantastic shirt at the mall but don't have enough cash to pay for it. After you save up for it and you finally get the shirt, you value it even more because you remember what you went through to get it.

Fasting makes you feel grateful for having food on the table. Sometimes we take full stomachs (and full closets) for granted. Experiencing the pangs of hunger may encourage you to be more charitable to the homeless who sit on the sidewalk.

Muslims are asked to fast for the duration of the ninth month of the Islamic calendar, the month called "Ramadan." The Islamic calendar is based upon the new moon each month, which makes it about eleven days shorter than the Gregorian calendar that is commonly used in America today. What does that mean for Muslims? It basically means that the month of Ramadan begins eleven days earlier each year. (It's pretty easy to fast in the winter months, when the days are short, but definitely a challenge in the summertime with its long, hot days.)

Does that mean Muslims fast the entire *month*? No. There wouldn't be too many Muslims left standing if that were the case. No one could survive a month without any food or drink! The fast is held during daylight hours. Muslims fast from dawn to sunset each day. People who are traveling, ill, or unable to fast are exempted, as are children, pregnant women, and those who are nursing their babies. God is not asking Muslims to fast as a punishment for their sins. Instead, fasting is seen as a physical and spiritual cleansing, as well as a test of will power, fortitude, and determination. In addition, a successful fast requires not only giving up food and drink (yes, that includes water and gum), but also the cessation of all bad habits such as gossiping, angry words due to impatience, laziness (sorry, but you can't use hunger as an excuse to get out of homework or cleaning your room!), and cigarettes (a great time to give up smoking), etc. It recharges your spiritual battery. Try it; it's not that difficult once you put your mind to it.

Muslims all over the world enjoy the celebration called "Eid al-Fitr," which is the festival at the end of the month of Ramadan. Again, when the festival occurs is determined by the sighting of the new moon, which leads to much anticipation and excitement since the uncertainty caused by the sighting, or lack thereof, leaves the Muslim community in suspense until the very last moment. Eid is a joyous day during which Muslims may gather together in congregational prayer in the morning—usually in festive, new clothes—and followed by visiting friends and family, and enjoying a wonderful meal. Children traditionally receive gifts of money, clothes, and toys, so make sure you're in the social loop since the Muslim definition of a child can easily include young adults in their thirties! Let your neighbors know about your annual event by decorating your house with lights, garlands, and paper chains. Just because your house may not be festooned with red and green during Christmas doesn't mean that you don't enjoy your holidays! Share your traditions with your school—They'll appreciate learning something new about you. Even if your ancestors came over on the *Mayflower*, you can share stories of how Muslims in different countries celebrate Eid. No matter how American you are, everyone loves a party!

The recipes on the next page can be enjoyed at any time of the year, not just during Ramadan. While most people focus on food as the primary issue in Ramadan, don't forget that it's much more than a month of deprivation. You can seize this opportunity to experiment in the kitchen by unleashing the chef within. Have fun!

Ramadan Dos and Don'ts

Do eat a healthy, hearty, filling *suhoor/sehri* (breakfast) before sunrise.

Do drink plenty of water, juice, water, coffee, water, and more water before you begin your fast!

Do try to fast for as many days as possible. God will reward your good intentions.

Do go to sleep early so that you can get up early the next morning and eat!

Don't forget to wake up and eat!

Don't eat in front of other people who are fasting. It's impolite.

Don't forget to thank God for the delicious meal you enjoy at *iftar* (the meal you have at sunset). Some poor people may not even have that luxury.

Cheesy Quesadillas:

Quick and tasty (did we mention easy?)

4 tortillas

1/2   cup grated cheese, or a couple of slices
of cheese (Colby-Jack or Muenster is
perfect), per quesadilla . . . or more if
you really love cheese

1/3   cup salsa per quesadilla

Fresh or pickled jalapeños,
chopped; to taste (yum!)

Method: Place cheese on a tortilla, top with salsa and jalapeños, then broil in a toaster oven or cook in a microwave until cheese bubbles (hopefully not till the cheese splatters all over the walls and ceiling of the microwave). Fold in half and enjoy.

Express Pizza

Mama mia! Your family will wonder if you're Italian. . . . This recipe makes two hand-stretched pizzas, about eight-inches wide.

1   ball unbaked pizza dough (store
bought is fine)

1   cup grated cheese of your choice
(Muenster works great) per pizza

*Assorted toppings of your choice: sliced onions,
beef salami, sun-dried tomatoes, etc.*

Method: Preheat oven to 425 degrees. Split the dough into two equal pieces, and stretch each segment to desired shape and thickness. Place each pizza on a baking sheet. Top the pizzas with cheese and toppings, bake for 10 minutes, and voilà! (Be careful! They'll be hot!)

Sinful Smoothies

Delicious and low fat—What more could you ask for?
(This recipe makes one serving.)

1/2   cup assorted fruit of your choice (berries, bananas, peaches, etc.), fresh or frozen, chopped

1   cup apple juice, 7-Up, milk, yogurt, or sorbet (or any combination of liquids. Experiment to find the combo you like best.)

Method: Place fruit in blender, add your one cup of liquid, pop on the lid, and whiz till smooth and slurpable. Add more liquid if you like your smoothies thinner (and drinkable!). Heavenly!

These recipes aren't specifically limited to Ramadan, so enjoy them whenever the mood strikes you—unleash the inner chef within!

Breakfasts

1. Leftovers. Heat up spaghetti, curry/rice, or stew . . .
Basically whatever you enjoyed from *iftar*! Claim
it before someone else in the family says, "Guess
what I'm going to have for breakfast today. . . ."

2. Eggs, any style.

3. Hot oatmeal, especially if Ramadan falls during the
winter. It'll keep you warm and full for hours.

4. Pita bread with cheese, hummus, or assorted dips.
It's quick, easy, and delicious.

5. Fruit/yogurt/granola, especially if your parents are
nagging that you're not eating enough fruit during
Ramadan because of all the baklava, cakes, and
pastries on offer for dessert each night.

Dinners

1. Ethnic/family specialty, which only appears on
your dinner table during Ramadan—especially if
your grandma is around to cook!

2. A potluck, where you get to sample a variety of
different dishes—and you know who the best cooks
are . . .

3. Any restaurant that promptly brings your food, so that you're not left raiding other people's bread baskets when it's time to break your fast.

4. Your favorite meal, which your mom/dad/ grandparents will cook once during Ramadan, to make you feel especially loved.

5. The late-night pizza/burger/ice-cream run, which somehow only happens during Ramadan because your schedule is so unusual, anyway. Plus, if it's the weekend, you can always go back to sleep after waking up for breakfast the next day.

Q & A

Q: Why is the month of Ramadan celebrated at different times every year?

A: Guess you skipped the beginning of this chapter . . . Muslims follow the Islamic calendar, which is based on the lunar cycle. It's approximately eleven days shorter than the Gregorian calendar, which means all Islamic festivals move forward, in relation to the Western calendar, eleven days each year.

Q: Am I allowed to swallow spit, brush my teeth, or rinse my mouth while I'm fasting?

A: Please do! While some people feel strongly about

these issues, use common sense as your guide. God knows what your intentions are. Don't stress if you accidentally swallow some water while brushing your teeth. Your friends and family will thank you for following some basic dental hygiene guidelines. In other words, *brush*!

Q: Do I have to break my fast with a date? (The fruit, not a boyfriend/girlfriend . . . We'll get to that topic later.)

A: It is customary for Muslims to break their fast by eating a date because that is how the Prophet Muhammad broke his fast. The sugar is easily digested, and boosts the low blood sugar that results from fasting. However, if you can't find a date, or don't like them, eat whatever you like. You're celebrating completing your fast, not punishing yourself with boiled Brussels sprouts and liver!

Calling All Teens:
Do You Guys Really Fast?

M. Mannan, age 12, Texas: "Yes, every day of Ramadan. I started when I was nine."

Julia, age 12, Arizona: "Yes, not a lot, but this year I'm going to try to fast for the whole month."

Esra, age 12, Illinois: "Sometimes. My mom thinks I'll get sick from not eating for a longtime. I like fasting and want to do it. I began last year."

Anonymous, age 16, Illinois: "Yes, I do, but only on weekends because of school during the week."

Some Ideas of how to **Celebrate Eid**

- ❀ Decorate your house with lights
- ❀ Decorate your hands with *mehndi*
- ❀ Buy presents for your friends and family (and drop hints about what you'd like!)
- ❀ Prepare festive dishes, or splurge on a special meal in a fancy restaurant
- ❀ Buy new clothes to wear to all the Eid parties and celebrations
- ❀ Donate new clothes/food to the needy, so that they can celebrate, too
- ❀ Have a class party and share your holiday traditions with your school
- ❀ Host an interfaith gathering to discuss everyone's different holidays
- ❀ Make Eid cards (when was the last time you used Elmer's glue and construction paper?)
- ❀ Play upbeat, festive music from around the world to put you in the Eid mood
- ❀ *Have fun!*

Chapter 6

Hajj:
The **Ultimate** Road Trip

"Announce the Pilgrimage to the people.
They will come to you on foot and riding
along distant roads
On lean and slender beasts."

—Quran, 22:27

Imagine millions of strangers gathered together, shoulder to shoulder, in one place for one common purpose. What could possibly unite them in such a mass gathering of single-minded devotion? It's the belief they are following in the footsteps of Prophet Muhammad (who was himself following in the footsteps of the venerable Prophet Abraham and his son Ishmael) in circumambulating the Kaabah and performing the sacred rites of the pilgrimage called "Hajj." The Hajj is the annual journey to visit the Kaabah in Mecca, Saudi Arabia. The pilgrimage takes place on the eighth, ninth, and tenth days of the twelfth month of the Islamic lunar calendar. More than three million Muslims gather each year to perform the Hajj, making it the single largest religious gathering

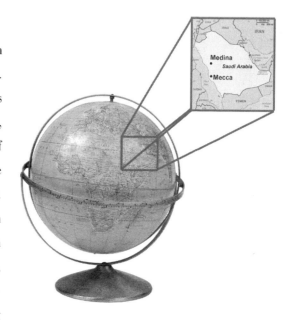

anywhere in the world. In the words of Syed Aftab Azim's classic book on Hajj entitled *On the Way to Holy Sanctuary*:

> *"Realize that for full twenty-three years, the Holy Quran had been descending upon the atmosphere of the historic land on which you are about to set foot, and that the fragrance, to this day, permeates the air that blows there. . . ."*

Most Muslims aspire to visit the Kaabah during Hajj, thus fulfilling their obligation to perform Hajj as it is stated in the Quran. However, if you are financially, physically, or otherwise unable to perform Hajj, you are excused from this ritual without incurring any penalty or being considered any less of a Muslim in the eyes of

God. Just as a journey involves planning and preparation, performing the Hajj is as much a spiritual journey as it is a physical one. While some Muslims feel they've reached their spiritual peak while performing Hajj, others find deep satisfaction in going about their daily lives quietly fulfilling their Muslim duties.

The Steps of Hajj:
An Overview

1. Be a Muslim who is physically and financially capable of the trip.
2. Wear *ihram* (two pieces of unstitched cloth for men, or a modest dress that completely covers the head and body for women). Wearing simple clothing emphasizes the spiritual equality of all the pilgrims. There is no distinction based upon fame, wealth, or power.
3. *Tawaf* ("turning," or circumambulation—by circling the Kaabah counterclockwise seven times).
4. *Multazam* (recommended prayer).
5. *Maqam Ibrahim* (pray and remember Prophet Abraham).
6. Well of Zamzam (drink the water from the well).
7. *Sa'i* (walk briskly between the hills of Safa and Marwah).
8. *Halq/Taqsir* (shave head or cut off a piece of hair).
9. Mina (stay in a tent for one day in the Mina Valley).
10. Plain of Arafat (remain for one day to commemorate Prophet Muhammad's Last Sermon).

11. Muzdalifah (spend one night out in the open in Muzdalifah).

12. Return to Mina (throw pebbles at three stone pillars that represent the devil).

13. Sacrifice (sacrifice a lamb, or pay to have the sacrifice performed).

14. Return to Mecca, bathe, and wear everyday clothes, and perform final *tawaf*.

Don't let this step-by-step guide fool you. Hajj is not just a to-do list, but a journey filled with mystery and grandeur. Every Muslim who has ever completed a Hajj is at a loss for words to describe the multitude of emotions they felt during their stay in Mecca, Saudi Arabia. Michael Wolfe's book *The Hadj* attempts to capture the magic of the experience in the following passage: "One had to perform the *tawaf* to comprehend it. . . . Orbiting shoulder to shoulder with so many others induced in the end an open heart and a mobile point of view."

Doing Hajj??

With more than one hundred and fifty responses to this one question, 99.4% of the American Muslim teenagers we surveyed answered with a resounding "Yes!" (Actually the responses varied from a luke-warm "Kinda" to a more emphatic "Yes, definitely," but they were all overwhelmingly in the affirmative.) Interesting, isn't it? Many teens may have difficulty performing the required daily prayers or annual fasts, but when it comes to their intention to visit Mecca and perform Hajj, they all feel the desire to worship at the Kaabah at least once in their lives.

Test Your Islamic IQ

(Relax! This test doesn't count, but it may help you on *Who Wants to Be a Millionaire?*)

1. The star and crescent are the symbols of Islam because:

a) The cross was already taken.

b) The star represents the guidance of Islam while the crescent moon illuminates the path of the believer through the darkness.

c) It looks cool waving on a flag!

2. The Prophet Muhammad received the first revelation of the Quran in:

    a) The Cave of Wonders

    b) The Cave of Ali Baba (that "Open Sesame" one)

    c) The Cave of Hira

3. The first *surah* revealed to the Prophet Muhammad was the:

    a) Surah Iqra, or Al-Alaq

    b) Surah Fatihah (after all, it is the opening of the Quran)

    c) Surah al-Ikhlas (it's the first one I memorized!)

4. Which angel first spoke to the Prophet Muhammad?

    a) Angel Gibrail (Gabriel)

    b) Angel of Mercy

    c) Angel on top of a Christmas tree

5. What is the Kaabah?

    a) The first house dedicated to the worship of one God

    b) The largest mosque in the world

    c) The study of Jewish mysticism

6. In which direction do you pray?

    a) North

    b) Toward the Kaabah

    c) Toward Disneyland

7. What is celebrated during Eid al-Adha?

a) Prophet Abraham's willingness to obey God by sacrificing his son Ishmael.

b) The completion of the month of Ramadan

c) President George Washington's birthday

8. How many pillars does Islam have?

a) Zero. How can a religion have pillars?

b) What do you mean . . . pillars?

c) Five

9. How often should you do Hajj?

a) As often as you can. Hey, who wouldn't want to vacation in a warm, sunny place?!

b) Never. Your grandfather already did it, so your family is exempt.

c) At least once in your life if you're physically and financially able.

10. When you perform Hajj, how many times do you circle the Kaabah?

a) Seven. It's a lucky number.

b) As many times as you can. After all, who knows when you'll return?!

c) Seven, because that's how many times the Prophet Muhammad circled the Kaabah.

Scoring:

1.	a) 2	b) 3	c) 1
2.	a) 2	b) 1	c) 3
3.	a) 3	b) 2	c) 1
4.	a) 3	b) 2	c) 1
5.	a) 3	b) 1	c) 2
6.	a) 2	b) 3	c) 1
7.	a) 3	b) 2	c) 1
8.	a) 2	b) 1	c) 3
9.	a) 1	b) 2	c) 3
10.	a) 2	b) 1	c) 3

What's It All Mean?

24–30 points:

> Congratulations! You're a proud, confident, knowledgeable teen—Great job! Don't neglect the other aspects of Islam, though. Being a Muslim is more than just knowing Islamic history.

15–23 points:

> Good work, but you still have some learning to do.

0–15 points:

> Where have you been? Turn off the TV and run, don't walk, to your nearest Islamic school for some serious studying!

> "He has laid down for you the (same) way of life and belief which He was commended to Noah . . . and which We had bequeathed to Abraham, Moses, and Jesus."
>
> —Quran, 42:13

The Quran

Chapter 7

Islam's Holy Book

"This Qur'an is not such (a writ) as could be composed
by anyone but God.
It confirms what has been revealed before,
and is an exposition of (Heaven's) law.
Without any doubt it's from the Lord of all the worlds."

—Quran, 10:37

*T*he Quran, or Koran, is the holy book for Muslims,
just as the Torah is for Jews and the Bible is for Christians.
Muslims believe it was revealed to Prophet Muhammad
by Angel Gibrail (Gabriel) during a period of twenty-three years,
beginning in AD 610. "Quran" literally means "the recitation," since
it was revealed orally. Verses were written down and memorized as
they were revealed, but it was only in AD 650 that all the various
copies of the Quran were collected, compared, and the most

accurate one was preserved while the others were destroyed. In this manner, the original Quran has been preserved in Arabic up to this day—with not one word altered in more than fourteen hundred years! Of course, not all Muslims read Arabic, so the Quran has been translated in more than forty different languages today.

There are 114 *surah*s, or chapters, in the Quran, ranging in length from a few lines to almost forty pages. They cover a variety of topics, from the creation of the world, of Heaven, and of Hell; to the Day of Judgment; to legal issues such as marriage, divorce, inheritance, and the rights of orphans; to fables and stories of prophets, which would be familiar to Jews and Christians, including the stories of Adam and Eve, Noah, and Moses. The chapters are arranged in order of length, with the longest ones at the beginning and the shortest ones at the end. Surah al-Fatihah is the exception to this rule as it is known as "The Opening" and is always the first *surah* in a Quran. In addition to this method of arrangement, most Qurans will identify where the chapter was revealed, e.g., in Mecca or Medina. This distinction is helpful in fully understanding the chapter by giving the historical time frame and place. Many *surah*s were revealed in order to show the Prophet the correct course of action, or to guide the community of growing Muslims in their quest for a righteous life in their worship of God.

Why is it important for Muslims to read the Quran? After all, it seems confusing, repetitive, and disjointed to the average person who tries to read it from cover to cover as a regular book. But that's the problem: The Quran isn't just a "regular book." However, if you view it as the holy word of God, which contains instructions on how to lead a good life in order to reach Heaven in the afterlife, then simply pick up a copy, open it at random, and read. Or better yet, begin at the end and read the short, early Meccan chapters first. You'll be amazed at the rhythm, beauty, and rhyme of the language in the Quran, and the eloquence and simplicity of its message will mesmerize you. The pursuit of knowledge is a requirement for all of mankind—most especially for Muslims—for the first word revealed to the Prophet Muhammad was:

"Read!" (Quran, 96:1)

True
or False?

Every Muslim has to memorize the Quran.

Trick statement. The answer is both true and false. Most Muslims memorize at least two *surah*s, including the first one in the Quran, the al-Fatihah. It's an essential part of the required prayer and encapsulates the entire message of the Quran in its simplicity and beauty. Most Muslims would also memorize another short *surah* as the daily prayer requires the recitation of two *surah*s. Many people never memorize more than two or three short *surah*s, while others memorize the entire Quran. These Muslims earn the honorific title of "Hafiz," which means "one who has memorized the Quran."

I have to be clean before I touch the Quran.

Another trick statement. It's true in the sense that you should treat the Quran with respect, and never place it on the floor, put your feet on it, or intentionally destroy it. Most scholars would require the state of cleanliness, which is required for the five daily prayers before approaching the Quran. You should ensure that your hands are clean, and approach the Quran at all times as a source of knowledge and guidance. This statement is false in the sense that while some cultural traditions require both men and women to be in a state of the utmost cleanliness and purity before touching the Quran, this approach would rule out many men and women who turn to the Quran on a daily basis but who may not be in a state of *wudu* (the level of purity required for prayer). Use your common sense, and try to be as clean as possible.

It only counts if you read the Quran in Arabic.

Absolutely false! Knowledge is knowledge, regardless of what language it's in. God made humanity in different colors, with different languages, so that we could learn from one another and appreciate, as well as overcome, our differences. While the original Arabic may contain beauty and poetry that can only be truly appreciated by a native Arabic speaker, there are numerous translations of great eloquence. Browse through a few different translations at your bookstore and select the one that resonates within you. While many scholars would argue in favor of reading the Quran only in Arabic, in this instance, follow the route that brings you closer to God, whether through literal understanding or spiritual transcendence.

I don't need to read the Quran. My mother/father/older brother/sister/cousin/uncle already told me everything I need to know about it.

False. That's great that your relatives are so willing to share their knowledge with you, but that doesn't excuse you from reading it yourself! The only way to form an unbiased understanding of the Quran is to pick it up and read it for yourself. Discuss it all you want with whomever you choose, but definitely read it with you own eyes and think about it with your own brain. Don't rely exclusively on someone else's explanations, no matter how well-meaning or wise they are—form your own opinion.

Teen Tips for Reading the Quran

- Find a paperback translation that you like and will actually read!
- Keep the Quran in your backpack or by your bedside table, so it's always handy.
- Treat yourself to a nice bookmark and use it, so that you don't lose your place and have to perpetually reread the hard parts!
- Talk about what you've read with your friends and family.
- Make up your own Quran summer reading program, and reward yourself frequently and generously!
- Get your parents to promise they'll throw a huge party in your honor if you actually finish it, and then read your little heart out!
- Ask for help if you don't understand what you're reading.
- Don't ever give up. It's okay if it takes you years to finish reading the Quran. It's still a huge achievement.

FYI

- The earliest complete copies of the Quran date from the ninth century, although fragments of older Qurans do exist, some as far back as the seventh century.

- The Quran as we know it today dates back to the collection of verses that Hafsa, one of the Prophet's wives, had in her possession and that she made available to Othman, the third caliph. After comparing her collection to the recitation of several people who had memorized the Quran, Othman was able to compile a single, accurate version of the Quran, which is the version Muslims all over the world read today.

Prophet

Chapter 8

Muhammad:
A Short Version of a Long Story

> "You are only a bearer of warnings.
> We have sent you with the truth,
> to give glad tidings and to warn.
> Never has there been a community
> to which an admonisher was not sent."
>
> —Quran, 35:23–24

The Prophet Muhammad was born in AD 570 in Mecca, Saudi Arabia. His father, Abdullah, died before Muhammad was born, and his mother, Aminah, passed away when he was only six. He lived with his paternal grandfather, Abd al-Muttalib, until the age of eight, when sadly, his grandfather too passed away. Muhammad's uncle Abu Talib became his guardian and raised him as if he were his own son. Although Muhammad suffered many losses during his childhood, he grew up to be a polite, respectful, and truthful young man.

Muslims believe that there were many signs that intimated at Muhammad's future role as a messenger of God. For example, it was the custom in Arabia for parents to allow foster mothers to care for their young children in the desert villages far from the pollution and overcrowding of the cities. When Halimah, a poor woman with few resources of her own, took charge of the baby Muhammad, her farm animals began to miraculously give plentiful milk for the whole family. The drought that had been plaguing her village ended, and the crops grew rapidly and abundantly. While Muhammad was a young boy, he met a Christian monk named Buhaira, who recognized several signs that the boy was especially blessed by God. Buhaira predicted Muhammad would have a great future and advised Abu Talib to watch over him carefully.

Muhammad grew to manhood and became a businessman. He oversaw caravans that carried goods for trade between cities throughout Arabia. After proving his trustworthiness and business acumen, his employer, Khadija, a wealthy widow, asked for his hand in marriage. He accepted and enjoyed twenty-five years of happily married life with her. It was only in AD 610, when Muhammad was forty, that he began to receive revelations from God through the Angel Gabriel. These revelations continued until the Prophet's death in Medina in AD 632. The Prophet was only sixty-two when he passed away.

Muslims all over the world respect and revere the Prophet

as the last Messenger; an example of the ideal Muslim; and, most of all, as the recipient of the Quran. As was mentioned earlier, the Quran emphasizes the fact that Muhammad was a man, not the son of God. His fallibility was a sign that no one is perfect; an important concept in Islam that ensures that while Muslims accept their limitations, they can also strive to follow the example of the Prophet. In addition to the Quran, Muslims try to learn as much as possible about the life and sayings of the Prophet in order to model their life after his. The sayings of the Prophet are called "Hadith." Approximately one hundred and fifty years after his death, several notable scholars compiled collections of Hadith after meticulously evaluating each saying for its veracity and chain of transmission. The actions during the life of Muhammad are called his "Sunnah," and many Muslims try to follow his example.

A widespread misconception among non-Muslims is the belief that Muslims worship the Prophet Muhammad. Nothing could be further from the truth! Muslims traditionally bow before no man. There are countless stories of Muslim travelers visiting foreign potentates and politely excusing themselves from bowing by explaining that in Islam, man bows only before God or while in prayer to God. While Muslims revere and respect all the prophets—beginning with Adam and ending with Muhammad—they are usually more knowledgeable about the Prophet Muhammad since he was the most recent prophet and many details from his life have been recorded.

Prophet Muhammad?

Prophet Muhammad was a businessman. He successfully led trading caravans across the desert.

Prophet Muhammad was a messenger of God. He received the Quran from God as a message to mankind for all time.

Prophet Muhammad was a husband. His first marriage to Khadija lasted twenty-five years. His subsequent marriages were contracted for several reasons: treaties with feuding tribes; removing the stigma of marrying widows, divorcees, or former slaves; demonstrating marriage as acceptable with "People of the Book" (Jews and Christians).

Prophet Muhammad was a leader. He created a community of Muslims in Medina with laws, rules, and charitable customs.

Prophet Muhammad was the Seal of the Prophets. Muslims believe that Muhammad was the last prophet to be sent by God.

Prophet Muhammad was a man. He was a man, not the son of God. As such, he was human and faced all the temptations and limitations any other man would face. However, as one of God's chosen ones, Muhammad was blessed with faith in God.

Prophet Muhammad was a father. He had three sons and four daughters, but unfortunately all of his sons died in infancy and all of his daughters, except for Fatimah, predeceased him.

True
or False?

The Prophet married more than four wives at a time, so all Muslims can too.

Trick question. It's true the Prophet was married to more than four women at one time, due to the standards for permissible, marriageable partners that he was trying to set. God states quite clearly in the Quran that no other man should take more than four wives, and actually shouldn't marry more than once if he fears he will be unable to treat his wives fairly and equally.

The Prophet Muhammad taught us how to pray.

True. God repeatedly asks us in the Quran to pray, but the specific postures and words are not stated definitively. The customary manner in which Muslims worldwide pray has been adopted since the lifetime of the Prophet Muhammad as people emulated his form of worship.

The leader of the Muslim community has to be a descendant of the Prophet.

Again, this is a trick question. After the Prophet passed away, Abu Bakr, a respected Muslim who was the Prophet's close friend and father-in-law, was chosen to lead the Muslim community. However, a group of Muslims felt that the Prophet's cousin and son-in-law, Ali, should have been the rightful leader since he was the closest descendant of the Prophet. This disagreement has led to the primary division in the Muslim world: Sunnis accept Abu Bakr and the subsequent caliphs as rightful leaders, while the Shias recognize only Ali (the fourth caliph) and the descendants of Ali as rightful leaders. Approximately 90% of Muslims are Sunnis and 10% are Shias. Sufis are Muslims who seek an intimate, spiritual connection to God through prayer, music, dance, and poetry. They can be either Sunni or Shia.

Hadith and Sunnah are as important as the Quran.

False—Hadiths (sayings) and the Sunnah (actions) of Prophet Muhammad are important to Muslims as they explain and elaborate on specifics, but nothing that contradicts the Quran is permissible. The Quran remains the ultimate authority and guide for Muslims, while the Hadith and Sunnah are useful as secondary sources, and aide to more fully understanding the Quran and the body of Islamic jurisprudence that has developed over the ages.

How Well Do You Know
Your Prophets?

1. Eve's husband was:

    a) Moses

    b) Abraham

    c) Adam

    d) Muhammad

2. Which prophet built an ark upon God's instruction?

    a) David

    b) Noah

    c) Joseph

    d) Jonah

3. The first female prophet was:

    a) Eve

    b) Mary

    c) the Queen of Sheba

    d) None of the above

4. Which two prophets rebuilt the Kaabah?

    a) Castor and Pollux

    b) Tweedledee and Tweedledum

    c) David and Goliath

    d) Abraham and Ishmael

5. Which prophet received the Torah from God?

    a) Moses

    b) Jesus

    c) Abraham

    d) Muhammad

6. Which prophet was blessed with extraordinary wisdom?

    a) Job

    b) Solomon

    c) Noah

    d) Aaron

7. Which prophet parted the Red Sea? (Hint: think Prince of Egypt)

    a) David

    b) Jesus

    c) Moses

    d) Pharoah

8. Which prophet suffered many hardships but never lost his faith in God?

    a) Adam

    b) Noah

    c) Abraham

    d) Job

Answers:

1. c) Adam
2. b) Noah
3. d) None of the above, even though Mary and Queen of Sheba are mentioned several times in the Quran as pious women who deserve respect and praise.
4. d) Abraham and Ishmael
5. a) Moses
6. b) Solomon
7. c) Moses
8. d) Job

Prophet	Number of References in the Quran
Moses	135
Abraham	67
Noah	43
Jesus	33
Joseph	27
Adam	25
Muhammad	5

Twenty-five Prophets
Mentioned In the Quran

Arabic Name	English Name
	Adam
Adam	Enoch
Idris	Noah
Nuh	N/A
Hud	Salih
Saleh	Abraham
Ibrahim	Ishmael
Ismail	Isaac
Ishaq	Lot
Lut	Jacob
Yaqub	Joseph
Yusuf	N/A
Shuaib	Job
Ayyub	Moses
Musa	Aaron
Harun	Ezekiel
Dhul-kifl	David
Dawud	Solomon
Sulaiman	Elias
Ilyas	Elisha
Al-Yasa	Jonah
Yunus	Zachariah
Zakkariya	John
Yahya	Jesus
Isa	N/A
Muhammad	

Halal and

Chapter 9

Haram:

Can I Go to McDonald's?

"O believers, eat what is good of the food
We have given you, and be grateful to God,
if indeed you are obedient to Him.
Forbidden to you are carrion and blood,
and the flesh of the swine,
and that which has been
consecrated (or killed)
in the name of any other than God."

—Quran, 2:172–173

alal and *haram*—**You've heard the words before,** but were never sure exactly what they meant, right? Basically, everything is allowed, or *halal*, except that which is expressly forbidden, or *haram*. So according to a loose interpretation of the above verses, when it comes to food, Muslims can eat freely except for dead meat (also known as "carrion"— rotting meat unfit for human consumption), blood (needs no explanation), swine (pork, ham, bacon, etc.), and anything that has

been slaughtered in the name of anyone other than God. The Quran mentions these specific food guidelines four times (Quran, 2:173, 5:3, 6:145, and 16:115), but it's not the only holy scripture to mention a prohibition on pork. References to pork as an "unclean" meat can also be found in the Bible in the following passages: Leviticus, 11:7–8; Deuteronomy, 14:8; Isaiah 65:2–5.

The first three categories are clear and simple to follow: pass on the roadkill and order your burger minus the bacon. It's the last instruction that gives rise to confusion. A strict interpretation requires meat to be slaughtered in a certain humane manner in which the throat of the animal is slit and the blood is allowed to drain from the carcass. In addition, the animal must be killed in the name of God, and a prayer must be recited by the butcher in order for the meat to be deemed *halal*, or kosher.

So where does that leave McDonald's? Strictly speaking, the beef or chicken is not *halal*, because it was not slaughtered in the customary Islamic manner. However, it was not slaughtered in the name of any other god either. In fact, it was not slaughtered in anyone's name. Since many Muslims are accustomed to uttering a short prayer or simply saying *"Bismillah"* ("in the name of God") before they begin eating, the widely held view is that this custom confers a *halal* blessing over the food. By thanking God for the food they are about to eat, Muslims remember God, thank Him for His blessings, and thus render the food *halal* in their estimation. The Quran also contains the following verse in regard to food:

> *"Eat only that over which the name of God*
> *has been pronounced, if you truly believe in His*
> *commands." (Quran, 6:118)*

Therefore, some Muslims residing in America, for example, are comfortable with saying *"Bismillah"* before meals, and then eating beef, lamb, or chicken in restaurants and cafeterias, confident they are following God's instructions in spirit, if not in the letter of the law.

Haram refers to the category of food and activities that are expressly forbidden in Islam. In addition to the guidelines for food, *haram* activities include drinking alcohol, indulging in drugs, and gambling. At first glance, it's obvious why these practices are to be avoided. Drinking can lead to a state of intoxication that can result in a loss of control of oneself or a car. Taking drugs is harmful,

self-destructive, and can expose you to the dangers of AIDS or even death. Gambling is a waste of one's money, plus most of these activities are illegal anyway for anyone under the age of twenty-one (so that definitely rules out all the teenagers reading this book!). Any of these activities in excess can lead to depression, poverty, or even suicide, so be smart and say no when invited to partake in the above *haram* situations.

Although the initial reference to these activities in the Quran (2:219) points out that there is pleasure as well as harm in these things and simply condemns them rather than forbids them outright, later references (5:90–91) instruct Muslims to avoid them altogether as they can lead one to forget God and definitely go astray. After all, our society wouldn't have a need for Alcoholics Anonymous (AA), Gamblers Anonymous (GA), or Narcotics Anonymous (NA) if it wasn't such a problem. The numerous substance-abuse rehab programs that are available all over the country highlight the huge problem that is currently facing America. Too many people are addicted to these harmful habits that not only ruin their lives, but the lives of countless others. Taking a serious look at these issues emphasizes the wisdom of the Quran when it counsels Muslims to avoid these activities.

Any college-bound teenager in America realizes the temptations to be faced in the years ahead of them. Rather than isolating yourself in your room or the library, you'll find that it is possible to fully enjoy the college experience—including attending sporting events, parties, and study groups—without engaging in any *haram* activities. For example, many non-Muslim teenagers have firsthand knowledge of the destructive effects of drinking and driving, or experimenting with drugs in school. College students are usually older and wiser than high schoolers (well, okay; that may be an overly optimistic statement!). This maturity should translate itself into better decision-making skills in college. So find some like-minded friends and be true to your beliefs. Peer pressure is only pressure when you are insecure or unsure of yourself. When in doubt, do the right thing. Remember, while you may fool yourself, your roommate, and your parents, you're never fooling God.

If people know anything about Islam, it's usually that they've heard that Muslims aren't allowed to drink alcohol. So how do you handle this restriction in an atmosphere where most people around you are drinking? Muslims believe that God has revealed His message in the Quran as guidance for mankind for all time, regardless of the changing trends within society. The Quran specifically mentions in 2:219, 4:43, and 5:90 that alcohol is an intoxicant—anything that clouds your mind or draws you away from the remembrance of God is prohibited in Islam. The first step in following this rule is to truly understand the negative consequences of losing self-control. You may be placing yourself at risk or causing unintended harm to others. If you think that drinking will help you escape your problems or impress your friends, think again. So while it may be challenging to socialize with friends who may be drinking, it's not impossible. Water, soda, and fruit juices are usually on offer, no matter where you are, and you'll always be popular since you'll be the designated driver!

1. Going trick-or-treating
2. Drinking flat beer (after all, it's not frothy anymore. . . .)
3. Eating a BLT (bacon,
   lettuce, and tomato)
   sandwich made with turkey
   bacon
4. Drinking root beer
5. Eating a hot dog
6. Chinese food
7. Oreos, marshamallows, and
   Krispy Kreme doughnuts
8. Pepperoni pizza

Answers:

1. *Halal*. What's wrong with some free candy? God never out
   lawed candy.
2. *Haram*. Beer is beer; avoid it. It tastes terrible, is full of
   calories, and will make you fat and drunk if you drink too
   much.
3. *Halal*. Turkey bacon is perfectly acceptable. Bon appétit!
4. *Halal*. Root beer is nonalcoholic, so go ahead and chug
   away!

5. *Halal*, but depends on what the hot dog is made of. Check the label. If it's all-beef, turkey, or chicken, you're good to go. Pass on it if you're in doubt or can't tell.

6. *Halal*. Chinese food is delicious. Just make sure your food doesn't have any pork or ham—especially in the soups.

7. *Halal*, but again, check the labels. Some doughnuts are fried in lard (pork fat), but Krispy Kremes aren't, so get 'em while they're hot! Some cookies contain gelatin that may be derived from pigs. Read the ingredients and use your own judgment.

8. *Haram*. As long as the pizza has pepperoni, it's *haram*—sorry. Stick with cheese or vegetarian pizza to be on the safe side, or check to find out whether the pepperoni is made from beef or turkey.

I Feel Alone When:

⚙ My best friend is talking about her date this weekend.

⚙ Everybody is going Christmas shopping.

⚙ Everybody is talking about last night's wild party (the one I wasn't allowed to go to).

⚙ I don't know all the words to a Christmas carol.

⚙ Everyone thinks I'm too different.

⚙ Sometimes I have to say no when I want to say yes.

⚙ I want to say my prayers, but I don't want my friends to think I'm weird.

⚙ I wish I had the courage to SPEAK OUT, but I keep quiet instead.

I'm Not So Alone When:

❂ I'm celebrating Ramadan *iftar*s with my family and friends.

❂ Everybody is buying new clothes for Eid.

❂ I get to eat whatever I want for *sehri*, (even spaghetti or ice cream at five AM!)

❂ Everyone is enjoying the Eid parties and celebrations.

❂ I know all the words (and even the tune) to "The Star-Spangled Banner."

❂ Sometimes I have to say no when I want to say yes, but my friends are in the same boat too.

❂ I'm surrounded by Muslims at Eid prayers, all bowing and praying together.

❂ I SPEAK OUT and sometimes people listen.

The Four

Chapter 10

Dating, Dancing, Drinking, and Drugs

"They ask you concerning wine and gambling.
Say, 'In them is great sin, and some profit, for men;
but the sin is greater than the profit.'"

—Quran, 2:219

id you turn to this chapter first? If you're hoping to find that Islam gives you permission to freely indulge in all of the above, sorry to disappoint you. Islam does forbid drinking and gambling (see Chapter 9 for a more thorough discussion of *halal* and *haram*.) The Quran initially refers somewhat ambivalently to drinking and gambling, as noted in the verse cited above, but it later forbids both habits outright (Quran, 5:90–91).

Basically, Islam takes the viewpoint that anything that intoxicates or interferes with rational thought is forbidden. Therefore, drinking, drugs, and, by extension, gambling, are all considered harmful, and should be avoided at all costs. All of these activities can contribute to the breakdown of the family unit, the dissolution of strong communities, and the downfall of many strong characters who somehow thought addiction could never happen to them.

Does listening to music fall into the same category? Well, depends on the person, the music, and the scholar. If listening to rock or hip-hop puts you into a good mood, then go right ahead.

But if listening to violent lyrics or suicidal dirges depresses you, then switch over to a more upbeat station. Use your common sense! Don't let music, or for that matter, any one habit make you obsessed. Keep your perspective—Listen to music if you like, but don't let it take over your life. Sure, your parents will probably yell at you to turn it down, so humor them. If you maintain a good balance in your life by putting school first and proving to them that you have goals, they'll be more likely to indulge your growing CD collection. Will listening to music automatically disqualify you from getting into Heaven? Of course not, but you have to use your head and moderate your listening. Does music lead to dancing? Dancing with members of the opposite sex? Is all this *haram*? Yes and no. There aren't many easy answers when it comes to these gray areas. Dancing in all-male/all-female environments is definitely okay (although it may not be the norm in high school), whereas dancing with members of the opposite sex is frowned upon if it leads to physical contact or suggestive moves. On this topic, you'll have to consult your parents on their views, and respect their wishes. Ask them to explain their stance. If you give them a chance to explain their experiences as teens and vice versa, it may help you to both come to a compromise.

Dating can be another taboo topic. Most parents take the easy way out and just forbid it. But what does the Quran really say on the topic? Unfortunately the references don't deal specifically with this issue. Men and women are equal in the eyes of God, and they should both respect one another. Marriage is stressed for many reasons, among them are the alleviation of sexual desires within the sanctity of marriage, the legal responsibility of the husband to care for any children born to his wife, and the general happiness of the community. Given that it's natural for you to want to meet your spouse before marriage, in order to make sure that you'll be happy, how can you achieve this without dating?

If your parents had an arranged marriage and expect the same of you, you need to sit down and frankly discuss your expectations with them, especially if they differ from your parents. It's not always easy growing up in an American teen culture, which places so much emphasis on dating in high school. Determine what's right for you and your family. Setting ground rules will help; communication is key to a happy, high-school experience with your parents. If you lie to them even once and they find out, you'll have to build their trust in you all over again. It could take months! So be open and honest and let them know how you feel. Dating should only be viewed as a preliminary step to marriage. If you're not ready for marriage, then don't date. It's truly as simple as that. Go out with your friends in a group—You'll have fun and won't get emotionally bogged down with a lot of feelings that you're not ready for as a teen. Concentrate on your academics, sports, and volunteer activities while some of your friends are getting sidetracked with boyfriends and girlfriends. You'll be ahead in the long run.

Help! I Want to Date,
But My Parents Won't Let Me!

Does Islam forbid dating?

If it is casual and could lead to premarital sex, then yes. But the Quran specifically states that a woman must agree to a marriage, which implies that she can get to know her future husband in order to decide. How chaperoned the setting should be can depend on your culture and your parents' preferences.

My friends will think I'm a loser if I don't date.

Hey, if they don't make the calls, they don't take the falls. Be true to yourself, but don't argue or try to convince them. Tell them that you're waiting for the right person to come along. . . .

How can I convince my parents to let me date?

Examine your motives. Do you truly want to get to know someone better, or do you just want to go out with your friends? Be honest with your parents and respect their views. Maybe they trust you but aren't sure of your date. Intentions are as important as actions in this case, so err on the side of caution by not putting yourself into a situation that you'll regret. If you just want to hang out with your friends occasionally, tell your parents and find a middle ground that you can both accept.

Is dating allowed if I stick to other Muslims?

Well, you're on the right track in the sense that you could potentially marry this person with little religious objections from your family. Dating between Muslims should theoretically be allowed as both parties will be aware of the physical limits implied in the Quran. As long as your parents are aware that you're not doing anything wrong and your intentions are to get to know each other better, with the ultimate goal of marriage in mind, then go right ahead (but please confirm with your parents that it's okay!).

Can I go to the *prom*?

Ah, good question. Most American teens agonize over their prom dresses, their prom dates, and their prom limos while many American Muslim teens are stuck wondering whether they're going to the prom at all! Debates on this topic hinge on two or three main issues that are red flags for most parents: the date, the dress, the dancing, the drinking, the drugs, the hotel room . . . Okay, there are a lot of red flags! Some kids just avoid the entire topic, because it's too much trouble to balance their friends' expectations with their parents' assumptions. Before you give up, try *talking* to your parents. Maybe they've heard rumors of the drunken mishaps from years past, but if they learn the prom will be thoroughly chaperoned, they're more likely to be comfortable with the event. Maybe they weren't allowed to attend their own prom, but they survived high school anyway, so they don't know why you're making such a fuss. Encourage your parents to get all the information they need from the school, your favorite teacher, or other parents who've already dealt with this situation.

Whatever the reasons, each family will approach this rite of passage from an individual perspective. Common solutions that avoid most of the red flags include attending the prom with a group of friends rather than a date, finding a modest prom dress for girls (although it's pretty easy to throw a shrug/cover-up over a ball gown), skipping the hotel room/unchaperoned after parties, and limiting dancing to friends of the same sex. If all these details are just too stressful for you, you can always opt out of the prom preparations and substitute a movie night with friends, an alternate Muslim prom with friends from the greater Muslim community, or even postpone celebrating the end of high school till after graduation. After all, the prom is just one evening in your life, not the make-or-break event of your lifetime, so relax. . . .

What Are Teens Saying?

100% of American Muslim teens surveyed will avoid drugs (smart thinking!)

100% of American Muslim teens surveyed will avoid drinking (un-Islamic and uncool)

80% of American Muslim teens surveyed think dating as teens is dumb

Yasmine, age 13, Arizona: "You're not going to marry the person now, so what's the point?"

70% of American Muslim teens surveyed think dancing is okay but only with members of the same sex—better to be safe than sorry—and slow dancing could lead to arousal, which could lead to . . . unwanted consequences.

Amira, age 16, Ohio: "Doing or participating in one leads to the others."

Naaz, age 15, Illinois: "All of them are wrong and are influenced by the American culture and media."

Maymuna, age 11, Texas: "I think people are weird to even try them. Dating, drinking, and drugs are dumb to try, but dancing is okay."

Random Thoughts About
Why I Love Being A Muslim

- I get presents (money) during Eid.
- Since Eid occurs twice a year, I get money twice!
- I can talk and confess directly to God (no intermediary priests or bishops).
- I'm helping the pig population by not eating them.
- The star and crescent are beautiful symbols associated with Islam.
- I've heard alcohol tastes terrible, so I'm glad that I can't drink it.
- I have fun being a Muslim!
- I don't have to eat dry matzo or fruitcake after religious holidays (Okay, I do have to help finish off the dry dates leftover after Ramadan).

"So ask for God's forgiveness. Indeed God is forgiving and kind."

—Quran, 73:19

Misunderstandings

and Misconceptions:
Are **All Muslims** Terrorists?

> "Say: 'We believe in God
> and what has been sent down to us,
> and what has been revealed to Abraham and Ishmael
> and Isaac and Jacob and their progeny,
> and that which was given to Moses and Christ,
> and to all other prophets by the Lord.
> We make no distinction among them,
> and we submit to Him.'"
>
> —Quran, 2:136

Islam **is the fastest-growing religion in America,** but remains one of the most misunderstood. Becoming knowledgeable about Islam is the first step in educating others about your beliefs, but in order to truly have an intelligent discussion about Muslim issues, you also have to be acquainted with other faiths as well. Patiently explaining some of the main similarities between your religion and another's religion is important, but seeing friends and strangers having that "Oh, I never knew you believed in the same God I do" moment is priceless! As the global community of mankind continues to shrink (thanks to the instantaneous sharing of information and ideas on the Internet), it behooves all of us to become familiar with other religions and cultures in order to reduce misunderstandings. There's a fine line between ignorance and racism, and confrontations are more likely to arise between strangers who mistrust one another's perceived differences than between strangers who are informed and educated.

So where does that leave American Muslim teens? Whether it's in school or in the workplace, you're sure to come across people who are surprised/bored/scared by your religious identity. Put them at ease by answering their questions honestly and openly. It's better to say "I don't know" if you're asked about a topic you're not familiar with rather than make up an answer that could cause more confusion down the road!

Surprising Statements, Simple Answers

Muslims worship a different God than Jews and Christians.
No, actually Muslims believe in the one God, the God of Abraham and Jesus, the same God most people refer to when they say "God." American Muslims may only have themselves to blame for this misunderstanding since most of them customarily refer to God as Allah, (the Arabic word for "God"). Among English speakers, it may be preferable to just say "God" rather than "Allah" since it will

reduce the confusion that arises when strangers insist, "You worship Allah while I worship God. I knew you worship a different God!"

All Muslims speak Arabic.

Again, the answer is no, even though most Muslims are familiar with common phrases, such as the Arabic greeting *"Salaam alleikum,"* which means "Peace be upon you," and short prayers/religious utterances, such as *"Bismillah"* ("In the name of God"). There's no requirement that you have to speak Arabic in order to be a Muslim.

Islam is a religion that mistreats/demeans women.

Definitely not. In fact, Islam is a surprisingly enlightened religion when compared to many other faiths, especially considering the traditional, sixth-century Arab society in which Islam first appeared. Women have the right to own and inherit property, vote, and seek gainful employment. In fact, women have been leaders of four Muslim countries (Indonesia, Turkey, Pakistan, and Bangladesh). Discrimination against anyone based upon race, religion, or ethnicity goes against the principles of Islam. While most countries attempt to treat men and women equally, in reality, women are as likely to earn less than men in a non-Muslim country as they are in a Muslim one. Discrimination really has very little to do with religion. It usually stems from ignorance, cultural traditions, or economic hardship.

Only Muslims go to Heaven.

The Quran specifically states that all believers will be rewarded with Paradise, and only God can judge mankind. Therefore, it's futile to speculate who will and won't end up in Heaven. (Quran, 98:7–8) According to Muslim beliefs, God is interested in pious, righteous people who do good deeds on this Earth, so if you give much thought to the afterlife and are worried about where you may end up, do as many good deeds as possible!

All Muslims are terrorists!

Sadly, after the attacks of 9/11, some people blamed an entire religion for the murderous acts of a few fanatics. It's morally wrong and intellectually reprehensible to blame an entire group for the actions of a few, so assuming you're dealing with a rational person who confronts you with the above viewpoint, you should be able to calmly state that Islam does not encourage or condone terrorism. In the Quran, taking another's life is compared to killing all of humanity, and murdering innocent civilians is forbidden in *any* religion.

While American Muslims endured heightened scrutiny and faced unwarranted suspicion in post-9/11 America, they also appreciated the benefits that came about through the education of the general public about Islam. Suspicions gradually subsided as individual Muslims went about their daily lives as peaceful citizens of this country, proving to their friends, neighbors, and colleagues that the hijackers definitely did not speak for the vast majority of Muslims around the world.

The history of America is one of immigrants pursuing their dreams in a land where freedom of speech, press, and religion are highly prized values. The Muslim immigrant experience has been challenged by what happened on 9/11, but this generation will be stronger and more integrated into the fabric of American society if they rise to the challenge of explaining to others that their faith should not be blamed for the extremist actions of a few men. The responsibility to educate ourselves, as well as one another, lies within each of us—whether we welcome this opportunity or avoid it all costs may determine the happiness of successive generations of American Muslims.

The Hijab

Chapter 12

Issue:
Unveil the Controversy

"O Prophet, tell your wives and daughters
and the women of the faithful,
to draw their wraps a little over them.
They will thus be recognised and no harm will come to them.
God is forgiving and kind."

—Quran, 33:59

erhaps no other single issue in Islam has generated more discussion among women than the issue of the hijab. Covering one's hair has become an identifying badge of one's "Muslim-ness," regardless of the intentions behind the decision. While only God truly knows what is in our hearts, many Muslim girls and women are wearing head scarves for a multitude of different reasons. "Hijab" literally means "a partition" or "a separation." Among Muslims, the term "hijab" has come to mean covering one's hair and fully covering one's body, leaving only the face and hands visible. What does the Quran say about the hijab? Interestingly, nowhere in the Quran does it emphatically state that women must cover their hair. Men and women are instructed to dress modestly and not display themselves showily or unnecessarily to others. In addition, women are instructed to cover their bosoms and not walk in such a way as to draw attention to the swaying of their bodies. So, according to the Quran, as long as Muslims are dressed modestly and behave respectably, no specific dress code is required. As an adjunct to modest dress, modest behavior is also encouraged. Therefore, ogling the cute boy in chemistry class or leering at the cheerleaders is definitely out! Needless to say, each person must read the Quran for themselves and form their own opinion.

The controversy over the hijab arises from a Hadith repeated by Aisha, one of the Prophet's wives, as follows in 4092 Sunan Abu Dawud: "Asma, daughter of Abu Bakr, entered upon the Apostle of Allah (peace be upon Him) wearing thin clothes. The Apostle of Allah (peace be upon Him) turned his attention from her. He said: 'O Asma, when a woman reaches the age of menstruation, it does not suit her that she displays her parts of body except this and this,' and he pointed to his face and hands."

In other words, her younger sister came before the Prophet in a semisheer gown through which the shape of her body was visible. The Prophet turned his head aside and said, "Only this and this should be visible," while pointing to his face and hands. Scholars have taken this story to mean that all Muslim women should cover themselves, leaving only their face and hands visible, even though most scholars also agree that this is a weak Hadith, meaning its transmission cannot definitively be accounted for.

Whether you wear a head scarf and fully cover yourself, or whether you just dress modestly, or even whether you wear shorts and a tank top, no one has the prerogative to judge whether you are a "good" Muslim or not. God is interested in the sincerity of your intentions and actions. While the Quran and the life and sayings of the Prophet Muhammad are there to guide you, only you can choose the manner in which you live your life as a Muslim. If you are more concerned about what is in your head rather than what is covering it, you won't go too far wrong. Islam stresses the inherent equality of the sexes, thereby encouraging you to view your peers as individual people based upon their characters and minds, not just as physical objects of sexual attraction.

Why Do You Wear Hijab?

1. My parents make me.
2. I think it looks cool.
3. My religion tells me to. I have to wear one if I'm a Muslim.
4. It's easier to be a Muslim when I wear one.
5. To be modest.

Farha, age 15, Illinois: "I wear hijab because not only does it cover your body, but it also shows how much you respect yourself."

Anonymous, age 14, Illinois: "It was rather a peer-pressure thing. Everyone around me was wearing a hijab, so I wanted to also. But now I know the full importance of it. It's to cover your beauty."

Fathim, age 15, Illinois: "I like people to talk to me for my mind, not my body."

Why Don't You Wear Hijab?

1. I don't believe that God wants us to cover our hair.
2. My mother doesn't.
3. It's hot and uncomfortable.
4. People will stare at me.
5. I don't feel that my religion requires it.

Anonymous, age 15, Illinois: "At some point I was going to start, but then I said to myself, 'Some people who wear scarves aren't always the greatest Muslims.' People who don't wear scarves can also be good Muslims."

Mannan, age 12, Texas: "Because I'm a boy, not a girl!"

Rabia, age 14, Illinois: "I believe that a person should pray, fast, and work on the inside before the outside. So until I lose my bad habits, wearing a hijab doesn't seem right to me. I would feel hypocritical. Hopefully I plan on wearing one."

Mehenaz, age 14, Ohio: "I don't think I'm ready for it. However, I respect girls who wear it."

Anonymous, age 13, Arizona: "Because God gave us hair—Why should we hide it?"

Be Honest . . .

- Do you judge people by what they wear?
- Do you assume someone who wears a hijab is more religious than you?
- Do you sometimes pretend you're not a Muslim?
- Do you choose your clothing in order to gain acceptance?
- Do you disagree with your parents on issues of clothing?
- Do you worry more about what you're wearing than what you're thinking?

Cultural

Chapter 13

Confusion:
Examples of Muslim Culture

"All that is in the Heavens and the earth belongs to God.
We had commanded those who received the Book before you,
and have commanded you too, to obey the laws of God.
Even if you deny, surely all that is in
the Heavens and the earth belongs to God;
and God is self-sufficient and praise-worthy."

—Quran, 4:131

hat is culture? (No, not opera or fancy French restaurants.) Culture is a reflection of the traditions passed down within a family, community, or country. It may differ from place to place, and there is rarely a "right" or "wrong" culture (except for certain reprehensible acts—like murder, rape, and theft—that are condemned in any culture). Culture can be as simple as the language you speak, the food you eat, the clothes you wear, or as complex as the way you celebrate your birthday or the way you handle a death in the family. Confusion arises when your culture (traditions) differ from your neighbor's and you can't decide who's right and who's wrong. Does Muslim culture clash with American culture? Is there such a thing as a Muslim culture?

As a teenager, you probably feel an overpowering urge to fit in among your peers. Safety lies in numbers, so you try to keep a low profile by dressing like everyone around you (all right, you avoid the goth look and ignore the unwashed, slob look, too), sounding like everyone around you (it becomes second nature to change your accent/vocabulary between home and school), and acting like everyone around you. Nothing wrong with melting into the crowd, but what do you do when you feel that everyone around you is doing the wrong thing? There are definitely times in your life when you have to assert your independence, especially when your conscience is beating you over the head and warning bells are ringing in your ears! Be mature and avoid the following actions if you can: cheating, picking on unpopular kids, stealing, gossiping, shoplifting, bullying, cursing to sound cool; sleeping around to seem cool, going into debt to look cool; stop worrying about trying to be so cool!

Behavior that is perfectly acceptable at home may be out of place at school, and vice versa. Maybe your family likes to enjoy their evening meal seated on a clean sheet on the floor, but don't try this in the school cafeteria unless you want footprints on your food. Do you normally dispense with cutlery and just dig right into your food using your fingers? Again, unless fried chicken, pizza, or hamburgers are on the menu, you probably want to pick up that fork instead of limbering up your fingers.

Confusion sometimes arises when you're not sure what to do. If you find yourself in a situation where you're honestly clueless, just look around you and imitate your neighbor. Stand up and cheer when your team scores a touchdown, even if you have no idea what a touchdown is. Sit down and keep quiet when your class is watching an educational movie (heckling the actors may be the norm in your house, but don't forget that you're in school now). You'll feel more accepted by your peers if you accommodate and adjust to your surroundings. That doesn't mean you become a clone of your best friend, but imitate just enough to fit in, without compromising your values or your identity.

Examples of Muslim **food:**

- Pizza and hamburgers
- *Shwarmas*/gyros (roast lamb/chicken in pita bread)
- Rice and curry
- Chinese food
- Italian food
- Fruits and vegetables

Examples of Muslim **clothes:**

- T-shirt and jeans
- Skirts, dresses, long gowns
- *Shalwar kameez*
- Suit/jacket and tie
- Shorts, capris, etc.

Examples of Muslim **languages:**

- English
- Arabic
- French
- Urdu
- Malay
- Spanish
- Russian
- Chinese
- Esperanto

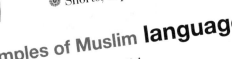

Dieu

БОГ

GOD

See the pattern? There's no such thing as "Muslim" food or "Muslim" clothing. Sure, Indonesian Muslims prefer noodles while Pakistani Muslims enjoy rice, but as long as the food is *halal*, anything goes. Enjoy whatever cuisine strikes your fancy. Don't label anyone (or yourself!) by the food they eat, the language they speak, or the clothing they wear.

Books For the Culturally Confused

Born Confused by Tanuja Desai Hidier: Hilarious account of a Hindu-Indian teenage girl's journey to acceptance of her own ethnicity in America.

Funny in Farsi: A Memoir of Growing Up Iranian in America by Firoozeh Dumas: Funny in English too! Read about Firoozeh's adventures in America.

West of the Jordan by Laila Halaby: The lives of four Arab-American cousins torn between Jordan, Arizona, and California.

Spiritualized: A Look Inside the Teenage Soul by Mark Healy: A beautifully put-together account of fifteen teens' spiritual journeys.

Dahling, If You Luv Me, Would You Please, Please Smile by Rukhsana Khan: Zainab craves a pair of Lucky jeans in order to be accepted by her school, but then she realizes that she wants to be accepted for herself.

American Muslims: The New Generation by Asma Gull Hasan: Nonfiction account of the challenges facing Muslims in America; issues include dating, marriage, and assimilation.

White Teeth by Zadie Smith: Culture clash in London depicted through two generations of Bengali/British families.

House of Sand and Fog by Andre Dubus III: Poignant memoir of an Iranian family's struggle to adjust to life in San Francisco.

Interpreter of Maladies by Jhumpa Lahiri: Collection of short stories chronicling love and loss between India and America.

The Hero's Walk by Anita Rau Badami: Mesmerizing story of an Indian family with branches in Vancouver and India.

Sister of My Heart by Chitra Banerjee Divakaruni: Traditional Indian values juxtaposed against the American quest for self-fulfillment and the story of how two women take different paths in life.

An American Brat by Bapsi Sidhwa: The adventures of a Pakistani teenager on a three-month holiday in America.

My Sister's Voices: Teenage Girls of Color Speak Out by Iris Jacob: An amazing collection of writings that sums up the issues we all face in today's multicultural world.

Does My Head Look Big In This? by Randa Abdel-Fattah: Engaging, often hilarious depiction of high school in Australia from the perspective of an Australian-Palestinian girl who has just decided to wear the hijab.

Are You Culturally Confident?

1. When your mom shows up in a traditional Indonesian outfit at back-to-school night, you:

    a) Run away when she calls you to sit next to her.

    b) Proudly explain what the outfit is called to everyone within a ten-mile radius.

    c) Do what you always do—chat with your friends until it's time to go.

2. Your Iranian cousin has just moved here, and he's attending your school. When he runs up to you speaking Farsi, you:

    a) Shut him in the nearest broom closet.

    b) Start up a long conversation with him in Farsi, too.

    c) Reply in English, and show him where the bathrooms are.

    d) You don't have a clue what he's saying because you don't speak Farsi—Your parents never taught you.

3. A television repairman has just come to your house while your mom is in the middle of cooking up a strong-smelling curry. As he sniffs the air curiously, you:

a) Frantically spray air freshener everywhere, including on the curry.

b) Offer to prepare a plate for him.

c) Decide that now would be a good time to slink off into your room.

d) Loudly ask whether your science-project concoction simmering on the stove is ready yet.

4. You're taking your relatives, who are visiting from a little village in India, to the mall. When you see some people from school approaching, you:

a) Dash into the nearest store—Never mind that it's the one that sells only Star Trek stuff.

b) Hold Auntie's hand while she *oohs* and *ahhs* over the neon lights, ignoring the curious stares she's attracting from your school friends.

c) Nonchalantly stroll away from your relatives and pretend to be engrossed in the latest display of baby clothes.

d) Introduce them to your friends. You're proud that you are able to switch effortlessly between two different cultures.

There are no right or wrong answers (well, okay, you really shouldn't lock your cousin into the broom closet at school!), but, in general, your answers probably reflect the level of cultural confidence you feel. Whether you're Jewish, Christian, Muslim, or an atheist, sometimes your religious beliefs will lead you down a different path from the majority of your peers. When you add the spice of a different ethnic or racial background into the recipe, the end result may be deliciously different.

Embrace your individual identity while acknowledging the validity each of us has to think our own thoughts, follow our own paths, and pursue our own goals. Most teens aspire to achieve success in their life—whether it is defined by money, power, fame, or peace is entirely a personal choice. Don't allow society to label you unless you truly feel that the label fits (do you even need a label?). You're a person, not a can of soup on a shelf in the grocery store of life.

Inventions

Chapter 14

From the Muslim World:
Where Did **Algebra** Come From, Anyway?

"It is He who gave the sun its radiance,
the moon its lustre,
and appointed its stations
so that you may compute years and numbers.
God did not create them but with deliberation.
He distinctly explains His signs
for those who can understand."

—Quran, 10:5

id you ever wonder who invented algebra? Or how people navigate ships? Or even how that watch on your wrist operates? Well, according to Islamic history, these are all inventions/innovations that arose from the Muslim world. Between the eighth and tenth centuries, the classical Islamic civilization spread throughout the Middle East, Asia, and Europe. While Europe and much of the Western world was passing through what is known as the Dark

Ages, it is universally recognized by scholars that the Islamic civilization kept the torch of learning alight in various fields. By translating, preserving, and elucidating upon research in countless fields, Islamic scholars played a critical role in Europe's transition from the Dark Ages to the Renaissance. Muslim scholars adopted the experimental method of testing their hypotheses and observations rather than the Socratic method that was commonly used at the time. Their achievement of translating earlier scientific works by the Greeks, Chinese, and Indians into Arabic enabled them to pursue innovative avenues of thought and original research. This preservation through translation furthered many of the theoretical sciences of medicine, astronomy, and mathematics, to name a few. Western European civilization absorbed this body of Islamic thought, and through subsequent translation into Latin and English, laid the framework for much of modern Western science and philosophy. The principles of scientific investigation, encouraged by Muslim thinkers, extended across many disciplines, beginning with art, architecture, and astronomy and continuing through the alphabet to end with zoology!

In AD 762, Baghdad became the capital of the Muslim world. It was a bustling city at the crossroads of the major trade routes between Asia and Europe. Scholars flocked to this city to offer rulers their services, to further their knowledge through exchanges with learned travelers, and eventually established the House of Wisdom. This institute's purpose was twofold. One was to systematically translate Greek scientific and philosophical works into Arabic, the other was primarily to serve as a research institution undertaking groundbreaking work in various fields. From Baghdad, knowledge spread outward into the rest of the Muslim empire, encouraging original thinking through investigative techniques in cities as faraway as Cordoba, Seville, Cairo, and New Delhi.

Al-Azhar University, founded in AD 975 in Cairo, Egypt, is the world's oldest university and remains one of the most famous sites for original research into the field of Islam. It concentrates on both the study of the Quran as well as the study of modern science. Countless other seats of learning sprang up in Syria, Spain, India, Turkey, and throughout the Muslim world. In addition to their many contributions in the sciences, Muslims also left a legacy of art and architecture still visible to this day.

As Islam spread, it absorbed a myriad of cultural influences it encountered. For example, mosques retained their overall simplicity of purpose, yet the addition of a dome came about through integrating Byzantine architectural traditions. Similarly, mosques in Iran soon included intricate tile work common to the region. The Taj Mahal is perhaps the most famous example of Islamic architecture in Asia, while the Dome of the Rock in

Jerusalem displays beautiful mosaics as a legacy from the earlier Greeks and Romans in the region. Islamic art ranges from calligraphy to textiles to miniature paintings, and can be seen in museums throughout the world.

"There is no compulsion in matter of faith."

—Quran, 2:256

Muslims and Their Inventions/Innovations

Abdul Hasan: Invented the telescope.

Al-Khawarizmi: Considered the father of algebra by many, he introduced the decimal point system.

Ibn al-Haitham: Called "the father of modern optics."

Ibn Rushd (also known as **Averroes**): Philosopher who is credited for introducing secular thought in Western Europe.

Ibn Sina (also known as **Avicenna**): Philosopher and physician who wrote *The Canon of Medicine* and introduced the quarantine that limited infection.

Ibn Yunus: Created a prototype of the pendulum.

Jabir bin-Hayyan: Called "the father of chemistry" by many.

Kutbi: Built the first watch.

Muslim mathematicians: Arabic numerals that advanced mathematics by replacing Roman numerals.

Omar Khayyam: Poet who popularized the quatrains.

Unknown Muslims: Believed to have invented the Mariner's compass.

The list goes on and on! These are just a few examples of Muslim contributions to our modern world.

Peer

Chapter 15

Pressure:

Don't Worry, I Feel It, Too

> "O men, We created you from a male and female,
> and formed you into nations and tribes
> that you may recognize each other.
> He who has more integrity
> has indeed greater honor with God.
> Surely God is all-knowing and well-informed."
>
> —Quran, 49:13

The community of Muslims all over the world is referred to as an *"ummah,"* a community. While the Quran specifically refers to the diversity among man as a strength, individual citizens sometimes choose to emphasize their superiority over one another based upon the color of their skin, their education, or their wealth. These arbitrary prejudices have no place in Islam, which stresses the inherent equality of all people. Muslims are taught not to pass judgment on one another as God is the ultimate judge of us all.

Teenagers face unique challenges and opportunities, especially in high school. The innocence of childhood, when friendships are based upon such simple factors as liking your neighbor's lunchbox or assuming that the person sitting next to you will automatically be your best friend (remember when you considered the person who ate lunch with you the most important person in the whole school?!), is replaced with more complicated decisions based upon appearance, wardrobe, and "coolness." Fitting in with the crowd becomes increasingly important as teens struggle to define themselves within their school community, their new *ummah*.

What happens when you feel like an outsider? Your religion may set you apart at times, but it can also provide you with the confidence to stand apart from the crowd and distinguish yourself in other ways. Rather than worrying so much about finding acceptance in a group with questionable values, surround yourself with people who share your morals. Join a sports team or a club that interests you. Above all, keep busy and motivated, and you'll find the differences you worried about may disappear as your peers get to know you better. By standing firm on issues that matter to you, you'll gain the respect of many people who secretly feel the same way you do, but don't have the confidence to declare their convictions.

All teenagers deal with pressure. Whether it's peer pressure, parental pressure, academic pressure, sibling pressure . . . Just talking about pressure is stressful! Before you throw your hands up in the air and shout "I give up!," take a deep breath, relax, and tell yourself that it will be okay. Sometimes the best way to cope with problems is to make a list:

1) **Peer pressure.** Try to make friends with people who have similar morals and values. That way, you're all comfortable hanging out together.

2) **Parental pressure.** Totally about expectations! Do they want you to cure cancer while bringing home a gold medal in *both* the Summer and Winter Olympics? Do you feel like dropping out of school? Communicate clearly, calmly, and . . . continually.

3) **Academic pressure.** Again, talk to parents and teachers, so they're all on your team. Be realistic, be organized, but above all, be yourself (no cheating, no ditching school, etc. You're only sabotaging yourself in the long run).

4) **Sibling pressure.** Does your younger brother or sister insist on tagging along to every social event? Or are you complete opposites, but your parents treat you like you're exactly the same? If talking to younger sibs doesn't work, a combination of bribery and begging ("I'll take you out for an ice cream/movie later if you just stay home now!") usually does the trick, but if it's an older sibling you're dealing with, the age-old technique of bribery, coupled with threats of squealing to the parents, have also been known to work . . . Not that either method is guaranteed!

5) **School pressure.** If you're the Type A person who needs to be in every club, sport, and theater production . . . Forget about it! No one can do *everything*. Prioritize your activities, so you have a good balance between work and play.

6) **Social pressure.** Are you worried about wearing the "right" clothes or having the "right" friends? Don't obsess over your weight or appearance. If your friends make you feel like you have to change in order to be accepted by them, make new friends. Also try not to be quite so weird/goofy/nerdy . . . A little bit of social assimilation can be a good thing in high school and college if most of the student body is fairly normal . . . Or make new friends.

7) **Personal pressure/depression.** Take it seriously and get help. If you feel like life is just too overwhelm-

ing, talk to your best friend, your favorite teacher, a school counselor, or your parents, but definitely share these dark thoughts with *someone* so that they can help you to see the light at the end of the tunnel. Any suicidal tendencies should be immediately addressed. Don't worry what other people may think—Your life is priceless.

Teen Solutions to Negative Peer Pressure

1. **Mentors:** college students/adults in fields that interest you
2. **Internships:** great way to investigate future careers
3. **Part-time jobs:** earn $$!
4. **Travel:** meet new people, see new places, experience new lifestyles
5. **Volunteer:** feel good about working while being unpaid and unselfish
6. **Study abroad:** immerse yourself in a different culture
7. **Sports:** builds athleticism, ability, and team spirit
8. **Youth group:** peer support, discussion, informal, and nonjudgmental
9. **Community service:** give back to your community
10. **Behavioral contract:** outline permitted activities with your parents

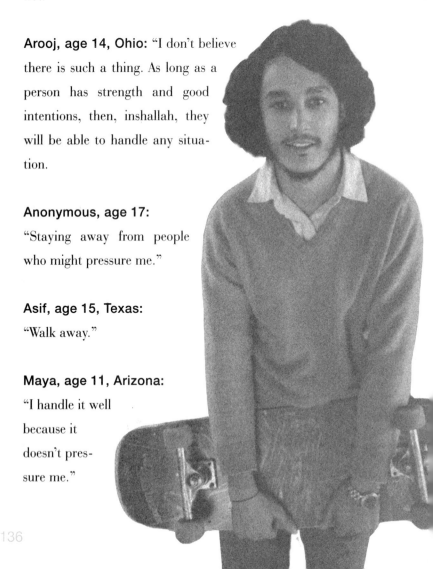

Fariha, age 15, Illinois: "Pretty well. I believe whatever is best for me, I will do. I can care less about if people like it or not."

Arooj, age 14, Ohio: "I don't believe there is such a thing. As long as a person has strength and good intentions, then, inshallah, they will be able to handle any situation.

Anonymous, age 17: "Staying away from people who might pressure me."

Asif, age 15, Texas: "Walk away."

Maya, age 11, Arizona: "I handle it well because it doesn't pressure me."

Some of Our Muslim
Teens' Role Models

- ❁ Prophet Muhammad, because he wanted to please God
- ❁ My mother, because she struggles to be the best Muslim
- ❁ No one
- ❁ Aisha bint Abu Bakr, because she was very clever
- ❁ My cousin Nazeef, because he is a very sincere Muslim
- ❁ Khadijah, because she supported her husband
- ❁ Malcolm X, because he empowered African Americans and encouraged a return to mainstream Islam
- ❁ Anyone who is better than me spiritually
- ❁ My parents and grandparents, because they taught me many things
- ❁ My grandmother, because she's very old and has a hard time moving around, but she never misses a *salat* (complete with *wudu*)
- ❁ Mr. Meyers (English teacher), because he's a convert and has a totally strong faith, yet he is normal and not all fanatical Taliban

Do You Think It's Easy Being a Muslim
In America?

No, because:

- ⚙ there are too many temptations.

- ⚙ after 9/11, everyone thinks Muslims are terrorists.

- ⚙ people stare at Muslims in head scarves.

- ⚙ I'm not allowed to do the same things my friends do.

- ⚙ the American culture is too different.

- ⚙ there are many racist people.

- ⚙ too much peer pressure.

- ⚙ too many distractions, like TV, music, movies, etc.

- ⚙ too much discrimination.

- ⚙ it's very, very difficult!

Yes, because:

- there's freedom of religion.

- if you fear God, you can live anywhere you want.

- we have freedom of speech while some Muslim countries don't.

- I have strong faith and lots of Muslim friends.

- I realize the differences between Muslims and non-Muslims.

- God will always help us.

- after 9/11, some non-Muslim Americans sympathize with us, too.

- a lot of people in America are becoming Muslims.

- in America, nobody really cares who you are.

- you can do whatever you put your mind to. No one ever got into Heaven without struggling!

- it depends on you, not your surroundings.

Islamic

Chapter 16

Interfaith:

Why Can't We Be Friends?

> "...To each of you We have given a law
> and a way and a pattern of life.
> If God had pleased He could surely have made you
> one people (professing one faith).
> But He wished to try and test you
> by that which He gave you.
> So try to excel in good deeds.
> To Him will you all return in the end...."
>
> —Quran, 5:48

One of the most important themes in the Quran is tolerance. Tolerance of different beliefs, different cultures, and the differences between individuals are frequently mentioned. But is that what God is really trying to say when it comes to people from different religions? Just to put up with one another? Or is He asking for something more, to truly accept that even though someone's path may not be the one you're on, you may still walk side by side for part of the journey? Some people ask themselves, "Why is an interfaith dialogue so important? As long as I don't persecute anyone for their individual beliefs, I should be okay, right?" A meaningful relationship with other groups is incredibly important, especially in a country like America, where diversity in ethnicity and religion is one of its greatest strengths. Furthermore, on a global scale, arming yourself with knowledge about the beliefs of others is critical to fighting against prejudice and ignorance—not just about your own faith, but about theirs, too. Many Muslims believe God has sent more than one hundred and twenty-five thousand prophets all over the world since the beginning of time, just to ensure that everyone got the message about believing in God! So before you make snap judgments about someone based upon their religion, first learn a little bit about their belief system. You may have more in common with them than you think (plus, most Muslims agree that only God has the authority to judge mankind).

Wouldn't it be great if the next time you heard someone say, "Muslims worship a different God," your Christian friend jumped in to correct him or her before you even opened your mouth? True tolerance and pluralism is when you hold the issues and sensitivities of others as close to your heart as your own. It is vital to speak out against injustice—every time and everywhere—and not just against yourself, but against *anyone*. There have been horrendous genocides of Native Americans, Aborigines, Bosnian Muslims, Rwandan Christians, and countless other people in countries around the world. The silence and passiveness of people worldwide during the Holocaust enabled the Nazis to murder millions of Jews without hindrance. But how do you ensure that the world has seen the last of these horrific human disasters? Becoming socially and globally aware through a meaningful interfaith dialogue is a good starting point. So the next time there's nothing to watch on TV and you're semiwatching some mindless show on MTV, check out the History or Discovery Channels for half an hour to learn more about the world around you.

No matter where you live in the world, chances are you're going to bump into someone of a different religion at some point in your life. Finding out that your lab partner in AP bio can't work on a Friday evening because he has to go to temple can be a terrific reason to ask him more about his beliefs. Similarly, don't be shy about explaining why you're skipping lunch every day . . . for a month! If your friends think you're secretly dieting, explain the mysteries of Ramadan to them or go one step better: invite them over to your house for a fast-breaking meal. Ultimately it's entirely up to you whether you take advantage of opportunities to share your religious beliefs while learning a little more about the religious beliefs of your friends. As long as you're not trying to force your views on anyone, you and your friends should enjoy hours—okay, a few minutes—of interesting conversations.

Faith is a personal issue, a personal perspective, and a personal journey. But can you go it alone? Well, yes and no. While your beliefs may be internalized, your actions often define your group membership. For example, some teens enjoy the solitude of reading the Quran on their own, while others rush to the camaraderie of Friday prayers. Some teens thrive on debating the nitty-gritty details of Islamic observance, while others are drawn to the big picture in

Islam of "we're all God's children." Since Islam is the youngest of the three Abrahamic faiths, it's fairly easy to strike up a conversation with Jews and Christians in particular, since there are so many common prophet stories. For example, you can't go wrong if you start a conversation about Noah—Everyone likes boats, right?

Wherever your beliefs lie on the spectrum of Islam, how do you feel about someone else's beliefs if they're not a Muslim? If you try applying the concept of pluralism to your view of world religions, you'll get to visit lots of different houses of worship, plus you'll find yourself enjoying more holidays than you ever dreamed of!

Religious pluralism implies the active desire to not only learn about someone else's religion, but the willingness to explore differences. If you're confident in your beliefs, then there's no reason to not have friends from a variety of different religions. Be respectful of their views and they'll respect yours. Of course, you're under no compulsion to participate in their worship service or do/say anything that goes against the basics of your beliefs, but interfaith dialogue is a wonderful way to learn more about your friends through mutual exploration. People are often eager to share their beliefs with others, because it reminds them of the loftiest ideals of their faith rather then dwelling on the inevitable squabbles within their own faith community (have you ever been part of a group of more than three people where everyone agrees?!). Imam Sabahudin of Phoenix, Arizona, often says, "You fall in love with your faith all over again when you try to explain it to someone else, but you just complain about the challenges when you're with others of your faith."

I Heard Muslims . . .

Have to kill all infidels?

No way! For a start, Muslims are forbidden to kill, unless in self-defense (like the other Abrahamic faiths). "Fight those in the way of God who fight you, but do not be aggressive: God does not like aggressors" (Quran, 2:190). "Infidel" is an outdated word from earlier translations of the Quran. A more common word is "idolater," which refers only to the pagans/idol worshippers who were actively plotting against the early community of Muslims in Mecca and Medina.

Aren't allowed to be friends with non-Muslims?

People who read verse 5:51 in the Quran "O you who believe! Take not the Jews and the Christians for your friends and protectors . . ." and think that God is forbidding friendship between Jews, Christians, and Muslims are mistaken. "Friend" is better translated as "ally," and its usage in this context refers to a specific historical incident when Prophet Muhammad and his followers were driven out of their homes. This is clarified in "God does *not* forbid you from being kind and acting justly toward those who did not fight over faith with you, nor expelled you from your homes . . ." (Quran, 60:8). In fact, the Quran clearly states that marriage between followers of these religions is permissible, so of course friendship is permitted and even encouraged!

Can't enter a church/synagogue/temple.

God created the entire world, so why wouldn't Muslims be allowed to enter a house of worship? The Quran states ". . . And if God had not restrained some men through some others, monasteries, churches, synagogues, and mosques, where the name of God is honored most, would have been razed . . ." (Quran, 22:40) and makes it clear that Muslims are required to respect *all* houses of worship. Observing a worship service of a different religion can be an educational experience. You may be surprised by some of the similarities between religions.

Want the whole world to be Muslim.

If we all believed exactly the same thing and behaved in exactly the same way, life would be pretty boring! Muslims believe God made us all different in order for us to get to know one another, not to convert one another. Islam isn't a proselytizing religion. "Do not argue with people of the Book unless in a fair way, apart from those who act wrongly, and say to them: 'We believe what has been sent down to us, and we believe what has been sent down to you. Our God and your God is one, and to Him we submit'" (Quran, 29:46).

Don't believe in Jesus or Mary.

This next verse from the Quran 3:45–46, probably answers this question pretty thoroughly!

"When the angels said, 'O Mary, God gives you news of a thing from Him, for rejoicing, (news of one) whose name will be Messiah, Jesus, son of Mary, illustrious in this world and the next, and one among the honored, Who will speak to the people when in the cradle and when in the prime of life, and will be among the upright and doers of good."

Muslims revere Jesus as an important Prophet and have the deepest respect for his mother, Mary, as well. She's the only woman in the Quran who has a chapter named after her. While Muslims celebrate the miracle of the Virgin Birth, they are strictly monotheistic in that they don't believe Jesus is the son of God.

World Religions
Pop Quiz

1. Which holy book contains the following saying? "Actions speak louder than words?"

 a) The Gospel

 b) The Talmud

 c) The Ten Commandments

 d) All of the above

 e) None of the above

2. Prince Siddhartha Gautama became the Enlightened One and documented his teachings in the sacred books of which faith?

   a) Hinduism

   b) Judaism

   c) Buddhism

   d) Islam

   e) Shintoism

3. According to Islam, women may do all of the following *except*:

   a) Own property and participate in business

   b) Divorce their husbands

   c) Personally accept or reject a suitor/prospective husband

   d) Marry more than one man at a time

   e) Keep all the money they make for themselves

4. Followers of the Church of Jesus Christ of Latter-day Saints (Mormons) fast how often?

   a) Once a year

   b) Once a week

   c) The first Sunday of each month

   d) There is no official Mormon fast

   e) Whenever they feel like it

5. Adam and Eve were banished from the Garden of Eden after eating from the Forbidden Tree. The angel who barred the gate of reentry was holding a:

   a) NO TRESPASSING sign

   b) Lightning bolt

   c) Shotgun

   d) Flaming sword

   e) A serpent

6. The two major Catholic fast days are:

   a) Thanksgiving and Easter

   b) Christmas and St. Patrick's Day

   c) Ash Wednesday and Good Friday

   d) Good Friday and Palm Sunday

   e) Catholics don't have to fast at all

7. Which Jewish holiday commemorates the story of Moses and the emancipation of the Jewish people from the pharaoh?

   a) Dreidel

   b) Sukkot

   c) Hanukkah

   d) Passover

   e) Purim

extra-credit question:

8. The summit of this mountaintop in Sri Lanka is considered sacred to Hindus, Buddhists, Christians, and Muslims because a footprint—believed to be that of Shiva, Buddha, St. Thomas, or Adam—can be found there. What is the name of the mountain? (Yeah, told you this was a tricky one!)

    a) Mount Lavinia

    b) Sigiriya Rock

    c) Adam's Peak

    d) Mount Pidurutalaga

    e) Mount Everest

Answers

    1. b

    2. c

    3. d

    4. c

    5. d

    6. c

    7. d

    8. c

If you got question #8 correct, then you're either from Sri Lanka or just incredibly well-read—great job! Otherwise you should give yourself a pat on the back if you got at least four out of seven correct, because most people really don't know that much about their own religion, let alone someone else's. But it's never too late to learn, as your teachers love to say, so don't give up, even if you got the answers all wrong. Just keep your ears and eyes open to the people around you. If you hear them mention an unfamiliar holiday, don't be afraid to ask them about it. After all, you'll probably have fun, make new friends, and hopefully do better on this quiz next time around.

"Whatever is in the heavens and the earth sings the praises of God. He is All-mighty and All-wise."

—Quran, 59:1

Post 9/11

How Do Savvy American Muslim Teens

Chapter 17

Survival Guide:

Avoid Extremism, Fanaticism, Radicalism, and Other Pesky "Isms"?

> "... But help one another in goodness and piety,
> and do not assist in crime and rebellion,
> and fear God ..."
>
> —Quran, 5:2

The consequences of 9/11 were especially harsh for most American Muslims. Not only did they share in the profound shock and heartfelt grief of their friends and neighbors, but they also found themselves under a microscope of social ostracism. Both their country and religion were attacked on that day. University of Michigan anthropologists Sally Howell and Andrew Shryock aptly sum up the American Muslim experience when they said, "In the aftermath of 9/11, Arab and

Muslim Americans have been compelled, time and again, to apologize for acts they did not commit, to condemn acts they never condoned, and to openly profess loyalties that, for most U.S. citizens, are merely assumed." This spiritually exhausting StairMaster of denial and defensiveness can potentially lead to alienation, but education and dialogue remain the best solutions to this quicksand of misunderstanding. Islam neither allows nor encourages terrorism, extremism, radicalism, or fanaticism, yet Muslims continue to be viewed with suspicion in an atmosphere of Islam phobia. Terrorists seek legitimacy by raising the banner of religion, but these extremists are motivated by misguided political ideology. The media's role in impacting public opinion cannot be ignored, especially if it results in widening the gulf between Muslims and non-Muslims in America.

Does religion foster extremism? How can a set of morals and values that aspire to raise up the loftiest qualities in man instead encourage him to sink to the lowest of evils? Religion has been getting the blame, but it's man's *understanding* of his religious beliefs that should be under the microscope instead. For example, out of the 6,236 verses in the Quran, less than 1 percent mention warfare as a course of action, and even then, strict conditions are placed upon the combatants. In Islam, Muslims are constantly reminded that God does not love aggressors; that war must only be waged in self-defense of life, liberty, or property; and that offers of peace must be met with the laying down of arms. However, passages from any holy scripture, when taken out of context or interpreted irresponsibly, can lead to a misguided justification for war. Islam is the name of a religion, and terrorism is the name of a criminal technique used by politically motivated groups, but in truth these latter groups are not representatives of any religion. Political radicalism often uses religious extremism to further its goals. There are those who resort to violence and hide behind the dogma of their religion, but they do *not* represent the vast majority of peace-loving people who practice their faith in obedience to God.

So, how do you respond if someone you know tells you that Islam is a religion that encourages violence? That's an easy one. Vehemently protest (nonviolently, of course!) their false understanding of Islam. No verse in the Quran can be used to legitimize the use of force to coerce belief or declare preemptive war. Entering into a dialogue with someone whose views are diametrically opposed to your own may be futile as neither side is likely to win the argument, but you can remain firm in your faith that Islam *does not* condone aggression.

For example, in the Quran, 5:32:

> ". . . *whosoever kills a human being, except*
> *(as punishment) for murder*
> *or for spreading corruption in the land,*
> *it shall be like killing all humanity;*
> *and whosoever saves a life,*
> *saves the entire human race . . .*"

If you hear arguments to the contrary, don't keep quiet since that could imply agreement. After all, if you were sitting in your chemistry class and your teacher gave the incorrect formula for salt (NaCL for those of you who regularly fell asleep in chemistry), you would raise your hand to correct him, wouldn't you? Or at the very least question him or express your doubts. Well, that's exactly how you should treat anyone who offers an extremist version of Islam to you. Force them to quote chapter and verse, *in context*, from the Quran, and they'll quickly realize that you're too savvy to blindly follow them. Why would anyone twist the meaning of a holy scripture anyway? Well, it happens all the time.

The Rhetoric of Hate

"We should invade their countries, kill their leaders, and convert them to Christianity."

—Ann Coulter, political commentator, 2001

She reiterated this stance on the October 4, 2004, *Hannity & Colmes*:

> COLMES: Would you like to convert these people (Muslims) all to Christianity?
> COULTER: The ones that we haven't killed, yes.
> COLMES: So no one should be Muslim. They should all be Christian?
> COULTER: That would be a good start, yes.

"They say, 'Oh, there's a billion of them,' I said. 'So, kill one hundred million of them, then there'll be nine hundred million of them.'"

—Michael Savage, radio host, 2008

"We—with Allah's help—call on every Muslim who believes in Allah and wishes to be rewarded to comply with Allah's order to kill the Americans and plunder their money wherever and whenever they find it. We also call on Muslim ulema, leaders, youths, and soldiers to launch the raid on Satan's U.S. troops and the devil's supporters allying with them, and to displace those who are behind them so that they may learn a lesson."

—World Islamic Front, 1998

"Islam is an evil and wicked religion."

—Reverend Franklin Graham, 2001

Hate speech exists, but it is rarely confronted. You can try telling the hate mongers, "Stop guzzling down the Haterade," but the best approach is to make the most of your own life by proving them wrong. Whether it's intolerance from outside your faith group or within it, everyone will hear outrageous statements with which they disagree. Informing yourself about the facts is the best way to defuse the situation. For example, some overly judgmental Muslims feel it is incumbent upon them to tell you that the way you pray, dress, speak, or act is un-Islamic. Any disagreement with them results in them branding you as a "non-Muslim." So what should you do? Listen politely, thank them for their concern, and assure them that you will look into the topic, while reminding them that God is the ultimate judge.

Teen Survival Tips

1. Be yourself. Your religious journey is your own spiritual voyage of discovery. Take charge of the responsibility God has given you and remember you are accountable to Him for your actions.

2. If someone calls you a terrorist, don't wait for an expert to come to your defense. Just remind that person that the fundamental beliefs of Islam are belief in God and doing good deeds. The killing of innocent civilians is strictly forbidden. Just like the other Abrahamic faiths, Islam emphasizes belief in one God, doing good deeds, being a good person, good neighbor, good student, good friend, etc.

3. If someone tells you that you're not Muslim enough, tell them you're more concerned about God's opinion, not theirs. Your own knowledge will make it difficult for others to distort or misrepresent Islam or intimidate you into isolation.

4. If the media's negative impressions of Muslims get you down, make your voice heard through letters to the editor, public presentations, interfaith dialogues, etc. Don't live in a bubble by alienating yourself from the wider community; stay involved.

5. If you're worried about "flying while Muslim," relax, smile, and wear shoes that won't take hours to take off and put on (clean socks are assumed)!

6. If you don't know how to respond to questions about Islam, empower yourself—try the library, the Internet, your parents, the Quran. The more you know, the less often you'll believe the allegations of others or find yourself clueless on the subject.

7. If someone calls you "un-American" because of your name, race, dress, or religion, remind them that you've been saying the Pledge of Allegiance in school on a daily basis! American Muslims embrace the values clearly laid out in the Constitution and the Bill of Rights.

8. If you want to give up because you're tired of being profiled, alienated, and stereotyped, don't! There's always hope for the situation to improve, so talk to others and get support.

Thoughts From a Young Muslim Man

I am an Islamic fundamentalist.

They say you should be scared of me.

They say that I am a radical.

That I oppress women

I have a beard

I don't listen to music

I represent all Muslims.

That I want to take over the world.

They say I want to blow you up.

They say . . .

They are wrong.

To me, being an Islamic fundamentalist
means being believing in God and doing
good deeds.

So where has all this misunderstanding
come from? Why do "THEY" hate me?

It's because they don't know me.

Afterword

The most rewarding result of writing *The American Muslim*
Teenager's Handbook has been the incredible and quite unexpected out-
pouring of support from Americans of different religions, ethnicities, cultures, and ages. Complete strangers have approached us following book
signings or presentations to shake our hands and thank us for dispelling
so many of their stereotypes about Muslims, stereotypes that they often
didn't even realize they were holding. The level of enthusiasm and thirst
for knowledge about Islam from the novel perspective of American Muslim
teenagers has been truly unbelievable, and we remain genuinely humbled
by this response.

"I wish this book had been around when I was a teenager" is the
most frequent comment voiced by Muslim adults. "Our faith could use a
book like this" is the praise from priests and rabbis. "Will you be writing
a sequel?" is a compliment that we are seriously considering. "My youth
group/Scout troop/book club would love to use this book!" is the feedback
that validates the use of this book as a resource on Islam. We include these
comments in order to highlight the diverse reception to *The American
Muslim Teenager's Handbook*, depending upon one's frame of reference.
Have we received any criticism? Where religion is concerned, people with
differing cultural and spiritual traditions are bound to disagree over issues
of interpretation, but these objections are rooted more in form rather than
substance. In our opinion, the few critics who disagree with our expansive
view of Islam are focusing on the minutiae of religious doctrine rather than
the intentions behind this book: to help dispel misconceptions about Islam
in an empowering, educational, and entertaining manner. Dialogue within
the family, within the Muslim community, and between Muslims and non-

Muslims are the desired outcome of this book. If we've been able to help just one person walk away with a more beneficial understanding of Islam and its place among the world's religions after they've finished reading this, then we feel we've accomplished our dreams. (Okay, peace on Earth is still one of our dreams, too.)

Writing a book about religion isn't easy. When we undertook this project, perhaps we overestimated our ability as well as underestimated the task, but we're glad we persevered. Deciding upon the topics to include in this book necessitated many late-night discussions about the importance and relevance of each chapter. Ultimately we settled upon covering the basics of Islam as practiced by the moderate majority of American Muslims. Cultural nuances are mentioned wherever possible, but, of course, the diversity within the Muslim world is reflected by the diversity of practice, differing levels of adherence to orthodoxy, and differences in interpretation. Teen-specific topics merited their own chapters, but could have been expanded into books in their own right as there's just so much to include in order to honestly depict the variety of teen experiences.

Whenever the issues became too serious, we made sure to insert a laugh or two. After all, everyone has a sense of humor, even Muslims! So whether you picked up this book out of idle curiosity or were required to read it as part of a school assignment, we hope it's been an easy and enjoyable read. In the final analysis, exploring issues of religion remains an intensely personal journey. In an ideal world, this journey should be traveled without fear of prejudice or ridicule from the unduly harsh judgment of others, and we thank you for allowing us to share our journey with you.

—Dilara, Yasmine, and Imran Hafiz

Glossary

(What do These Words Mean Again?)

Allah: Arabic word for "God"; the one God; the God of Moses, Abraham, Jesus, and Muhammad; the same God which Jews, Christians, and Muslims refer to when they say "God." Seriously, it just means God.

Bismillah: Means "in the name of God," a common term used as a blessing or invocation, i.e., before a meal, before beginning a test, or before a journey.

du'a: Arabic word for "prayer," commonly used to refer to any additional, voluntary prayer that can be offered at any time of the day or night, in any language, anywhere, and in any manner.

Eid: A festival, holiday. There are two Eid holidays (Eid al-Fitr and Eid al-Adha). Yep—presents twice a year!

fast: To abstain from food and beverages, from sunrise to sunset, specifically during Ramadan . . . Yeah, it's not easy, but you'll survive.

Five Pillars of Islam: The declaration of faith, prayer, charity, fasting, and pilgrimage to Mecca.

Friday: Umm, it's a day of the week . . . It comes after Thursday. Also the Muslim day of congregational prayer (like the importance of Saturday for Jews or Sunday for Christians).

Hajj: The pilgrimage to Mecca, Saudi Arabia. It's a journey that most Muslims hope to make at least once in their lives, if they are financially and physically able.

Hadith: The sayings of Prophet Muhammad.

halal: Things that are allowed, according to the Quran (anything that isn't specifically forbidden is technically allowed—that includes iPods!); often used to refer to food or activities.

haram: Things that are forbidden, according to the Quran (basically anything bad for you, physically or spiritually—the obvious ones being drinking, doing drugs, murder, stealing, lying, etc.); often used to refer to food or activities.

hijab: Literally, a "partition" or "separation." Often used as a reference to a woman's head scarf/full-body covering. Observance depends upon Quranic interpretation and cultural background.

iftar: Also known as "Finally, we can eat!"; the traditional name for the meal that is enjoyed after sunset, after a day of fasting during the month of Ramadan. "Is it *iftar* time yet?" is the most common phrase heard in Muslim households around the world during the minutes leading up to the *iftar*.

Jalsah: One of the prayer postures; also known as the "sitting."

Kaabah: A cube-shaped building in Mecca, Saudi Arabia, and the most holy building for Muslims due to what it represents: the first building on Earth that was dedicated solely for the worship of God. Built by Abraham and his son Ishmael, it is believed that the foundations were laid by Adam (yes, the Adam from Adam and Eve). Muslims do not worship the Kaabah, however, they do pray toward it, as a gesture of unity during prayer, in obedience to God's instructions.

Mecca: A city in Saudi Arabia that is commonly referred to as the most holy city for Muslims, due to the presence of the Kaabah and the fact that Prophet Muhammad's revelations began in Mecca. Also the birthplace of Islam.

monotheism: The belief in one god as opposed to the worship of many gods. Judaism, Christianity, and Islam are all monotheistic faiths.

Prophet: An apostle, messenger; someone chosen by God to pass on His message to mankind, or to serve as a reminder of earlier revelations.

Muslims believe five prophets were also messengers whom God gifted with revelations/Holy Scriptures (Abraham and the Scrolls, Moses and the Torah, Jesus and the Gospel, David and the Psalms, Muhammad and the Quran).

qiyam: One of the prayer postures; also known as "the standing."

Quran: The holy book of Islam, considered the word of God as revealed to the Prophet Muhammad from AD 610–633. The original language of the Quran is Arabic, but it has been translated into more than fifty different languages.

raka: A unit of prayer that consists of specific verses/postures. The obligatory prayers throughout the day consist of two, three, or four *raka*s, depending on the time of day.

Ramadan: Commonly known as "the month of fasting," technically, it is the ninth month of the Islamic calendar. A time of physical purification and challenge, spiritual renewal, and social and charitable activities.

ruku: Another one of the prayer postures; also known as "the bowing."

sajdah: Yep, you guessed it—another one of the prayer postures. This one is known as "the prostration."

salat: The Arabic word for "prayer," commonly used to refer to the five daily, obligatory prayers that are recited in Arabic.

Shahadah: The profession of faith, the affirmation that there is only one god and that Muhammad is His prophet. It's repeated during every obligatory prayer.

Shia: A denomination within Islam that makes up approximately 10 percent of the Muslim population. Following the death of Prophet Muhammad, a disagreement over the leadership of the first Muslim community led to this division between Muslims. Both Sunnis and Shias view the Quran as the revealed word of God.

Sufis: Muslims who seek an intimate, spiritual connection to God through prayer, music, dance, or poetry. You've probably heard of Jalal ad-din Rumi and the Whirling Dervishes, right?

Sunni: The name for the denomination within Islam that makes up approximately 90 percent of the Muslim population.

Sunnah: The actions of the Prophet Muhammad; the accepted manner in which he lived his life. Muslims all over the world try to follow his example of kindness, tolerance, etc.

surah: A chapter of the Quran. There are 114 chapters (87 were revealed in Mecca and 27 were revealed in Medina).

taqwa: "God consciousness"; the belief that God knows your every thought, action, and intention. A state of mind that leads to inner peace, through obedience to God's wishes.

ummah: The worldwide community of Muslims.

zakat: Loosely translates to "charity," but refers specifically to the annual alms giving that God asks of Muslims. Also, it's the concept that it's good to give a little bit of your wealth to those who are less fortunate, in order for you to enjoy the remainder with a clear conscience.

"God invites you to the Home of Peace."

—Quran, 10:25

Acknowledgments

We'd like to thank the many people who have encouraged us along this journey, especially Imam Subahudin Ceman, for his thoughtful perspectives; Sister Muna Ali, for invaluable corrections; Rabbi Charles Herring, for insight into the Jewish faith; and the numerous teens who participated in the survey. Thank you to Asma Gull Hasan and Dr. Jeffrey Lang for their wholehearted belief in this book and their guidance to American Muslims. Thanks to Ginee Seo and Anne Zafian, for believing in this book and for bringing it to the larger publishing world; Jeannie Ng, for her eagle eyes; Deb Sfetsios, for her beautiful designs; and the rest of the publishing team at Atheneum/Simon & Schuster, for their invaluable support.

We'd especially like to thank Hamid Hafiz, ideal husband and understanding father, for his patience and full-fledged support throughout this project. Most importantly, we'd like to acknowledge our parents and grandparents: Col. M.A.R. Ibn Hafiz and Begum Safia Hafiz and Mr. and Mrs. Bashir and Yvonne Karamali. They epitomize the essence of living a spiritual life and they continue to be stellar examples of the kindness, love, and open-mindedness that unite all faiths as one.

Needless to say, all the opinions expressed in this book, whether by the authors, the teens via the questionnaire, or anonymously, are no reflection upon any of the people or institutions whose names appear within these pages. We take sole responsibility for any errors or misunderstandings we may have inadvertently made.

Bibliography

Ali-Karamali, Sumbul. *The Muslim Next Door: The Qur'an, the Media, and That Veil Thing*. Ashland: White Cloud Press, 2008.

Azim, Syed Aftab. *The Pilgrimage*. Karachi: Pakistan International Airlines, 1985.

Cook, Michael. *The Koran*. Oxford: Oxford University Press, 2000.

Eposito, John L. and Dalia Mogahed. *Who Speaks for Islam? What a Billion Muslims Really Think*. New York: Gallup Press, 2007.

Haddad, Yvonne Yazbeck, and Adair T. Lummis. *Islamic Values In the United States: A Comparative Study*. New York: Oxford University Press, Inc., 1987.

Hassan, Asma Gull. *American Muslims: The New Generation*. New York: Continuum, 2000.

Lang, Jeffrey. *Even Angels Ask: A Journey to Islam in America*. Beltsville: Amana Publications, 1997.

Lunde, Paul. *Islam*. New York: DK Publishing, Inc., 2002.

Siddiqui, Haroon. *Being Muslim*. Toronto: Groundwood Books, 2006.

Siddiqui, Mona. *How to Read the Qu'ran*. London: Granta Books, 2007.

Wolfe, Michael. *The Hadj: An American's Pilgrimage to Mecca*. New York: Atlantic Monthly Press, 1993.

_____, ed. *Taking Back Islam: American Muslims Reclaim Their Faith*. Pennsylvania: Rodale Inc., 2002.